Hounds at the gravel pits, Chignall Smealy (Hester Davies Collection)

Mid Essex Beagles

1953–2004

An illustrated history

By

Peter Bostridge

Mid Essex Beagles 1953–2004, *An illustrated history*
By Peter Bostridge

Published by:
Julia Porter,
Elm Cottage,
Laindon Cottage Road,
Little Burstead,
Billericay,
Essex CM12 9TJ

First published 2006

ISBN10: 0-9554203-0-X

ISBN13: 978-0-9554203-0-6

Book design by Graham Land Creative Services, Wymondham
Printed by Norwich Colour Print, Norwich

For

Christchurch 'Wishful' 1953

New College & Magdalen 'Gossip' 1949

Newcastle 'Juno' 1955

from whom the Mid Essex Beagles laid the pack's foundations

FOREWORD

In every walk of life there are some who are outstanding for the effort, time and money which they put into their chosen vocation. Such a one is Phemie Angus. She has been the inspiration of the Mid Essex Beagles for many years, giving a number of people great enjoyment and the satisfaction which can result from the activities of a pack of hounds, apart from the actual hunting.

This book is more than a biography. It shows all the complexities of running a pack of hounds and the hard work which is required, never an easy matter. Written in a clear and entertaining manner it makes most enjoyable reading.

John Kirkpatrick

John Kirkpatrick was Secretary of the Association of Masters of Harriers and Beagles from 1956 until 1996 and its President in 1997. He was Master of the Trinity Foot Beagles 1948–50

CONTENTS

PRELUDE

It was a bright wintry sun that shone down upon an extraordinary sight. A grass airfield around which light aircraft taxied to the end of the runway as the last to land slowly turned off the marked runway blipping his engine and weaved through hounds tearing across after a hare. No one seemed to worry and the pilots casually watched as the hare made for an adjacent covert, hounds giving tongue behind and the huntsman and whips running with lungs afire to keep up. The scent was lost for a while and hounds feathered around the trees whilst the field caught up with them.

This was my first introduction to the Mid Essex Beagles, in those days a tri-colour pack and a wonderful sight to see in full cry. (One must not confuse the pack of hounds with the Essex Beagles, an athletic club founded in 1887 and with a long history of impressive runners including the famous Jim Peters.) I secretly wondered if these beaglers were all mad; with memories of Royal Air Force lore about precautions in crossing airfields it seemed suicidal, but try to tell a hound to go round aeroplanes and avoid runways and one is up against a difficulty. The scent is there, follow the scent. Anyway, it was almost Gallic in its charm. I was completely sold. Taken in hand by a rather elderly, stocky man with a thatch of grey hair and a ruddy face with longish sideburns, a pullover that had seen better days, and plus twos tucked into long socks that appeared to cover a pair of Queen Ann legs rescued from a sideboard, his kindly gruff voice soon put me at my ease as he explained the intricacies of beagling. I had followed foxhounds when I was at school, but never beagles. As a student I could not afford a horse and I realised this was one way to hunt without the need to be mounted. I could just about afford the 5/- cap. I noticed most of the field wore breeches with long socks and either gym shoes, old tennis shoes or hockey boots, the latter preferred. Most were clad in hacking jackets and stocks, the cognoscenti sporting jagged tears from barbed wire in all their garments. Despite the hard wear and tear on kit the

Master, huntsman and whips were looking very smart in their hard hunt caps and green coats, even if the white breeches and green socks were generously smeared with mud.

In fact, that day the Master was a lady, and so too was the young huntsman, Phemie Angus, who ran like the wind in a green divided skirt and occasionally tooted the horn which she carried tucked in the front of her tunic. The whips were somewhat aged by comparison but stolidly kept up, using their guile to offset lack of speed.

The year was 1956. We had met up the road at an old pub, The Rabbits, at Stapleford Abbots in Essex. It was a good introduction to beagling for everyone was very friendly. In the bar the Secretary introduced himself and some of the younger members of the field gathered around to put me in the picture. When hounds moved off I felt I was part of the hunt. They started over heavy, deep ploughed Essex clay and in ordinary shoes I was at a distinct disadvantage. Thank God for the walking stick I had picked up at the last minute. It was needed, first to prise my feet out of the bad spots, and then to scrape off the few inches by which my height had increased after a field or two. I understood a little what it must have been like in the mud of Flanders during the First War. That day the airfield was about the only piece of grass there was. I had hoped that they would hunt over the parkland at Albyns but we never touched that side of the road all day and in fact finished nearer Abridge.

Several of us made the journey home by bus at the end of the day. We sat upstairs in the front window, pleasantly worn but content with our muddy feet stretched out and our hands in our pockets, not talking much, but savouring each minute of the day's hunt. I think I must have picked up the meet from the Horse and Hound, for in those days meets were advertised fully with impunity. With no personal transport it was within easy distance by bus, rather a treck by bicycle and by the end of the day I would have been hard pushed to peddle. I had become a beagler. For 48 years I have maintained contact with the hunt and it

The Rabbits. Stapleford Abbotts   Peter Brundge 1957

was at a reunion lunch after disbandment that the idea of writing about the Mid Essex Beagles and their record during 50 years of hunting gradually took shape.

In many ways it was a private pack, for although a subscription was levied from those invited to be members and a cap taken from casual followers, hounds were never owned by the committee but by only three people throughout the hunt's history. Firstly, a Hornchurch greengrocer who had a few couple of hounds which he began to hunt with others owned by a retired Army officer who dallied with the importation of wines. Ultimately, the latter took over all the hounds but subsequently passed them on to Phemie Angus who still has the remnants, so it is not difficult to trace some of the present hounds right back to the original pack. It has always been Phemie Angus's ideal to produce a pack of hounds which will hunt together and give a good day's sport and this she did; unfortunately not all packs have been so successful during their history and it takes much hard work to produce an even pack with good noses, good discipline and the ability to figure out a line without riot, splitting or completely ignoring the horn. Every pack has its off days, but some more than others, and the Mid Essex were not among the latter.

One cannot write without a word about the farmers who made it possible for hounds to hunt over their land. They could have said no, but instead they were the best of hosts and put up with the followers tramping all over their fields and around their farm buildings, sometimes when they could afford the time joining in as well. It is a debt which will never be forgotten.

Peter Bostridge
Melton Constable
25th July 2006

CHAPTER 1

The Start of Beagling in Essex

Hare hunting goes back to early history, for Roman writers refer to beagles (canicula venaticus) and certainly small hounds are mentioned in Saxon writings. Beagles themselves were often referred to with affection in later times as 'jelly dogs'. Aesop's fable of the Hare and the Tortoise is a wonderful introduction to the hare at an early age. Lepus, the hare, has been with us in its mysterious life since time immemorial and since the 19th century has been hunted by packs of beagles, in Essex and many other counties. Dame Juliana Berners in her Boke of St. Albans regards the hare as *'the marvellest beest that is on any londe'*. She should know – she was, without doubt, the most famous all round field sportsman of the late fifteenth century. At the time of writing there are still 63 recognised beagle packs extant in England and Wales with others in Eire and the USA.

Unlike foxes, hares do not generally run in straight lines but often tend to run in circles, except towards the end of the season when they have gone courting and make a bee line back to their own territory if hunted. Beagles are smaller than foxhounds and bred to match their quarry, for although the hare can accelerate for short distances after being found she will slow down to a lesser pace later and often stop to listen, for her eyesight is poor, and perhaps will change direction from time to time. It is usually quite soon after a hare is put up by hounds that it becomes apparent she is either running left or right handed. This means that with beagles following the scent of a hare it is possible to keep up without the aid of a horse and, in fact, the huntsman and whips manage to do this for some hours whilst the field following behind can select a vantage point from which to view the hunt and benefit from the hare running a circle.

Whereas the oldest pack of beagles is, without doubt, the Royal Rock Beagles who began hunting the Hundred of Wirral in 1845 and were still hunting in 2005, in Essex the first to hunt beagles was Capt. Margesson of the 56th Regiment (2nd. Batt. Essex) who kept a military pack during 1861–63 at

Colchester. Then the Garrison Beagles, a subscription pack of 14 hounds, hunted during 1871 for two seasons with a gap until 1875/6 season when the 7th Royal Fusiliers put together a pack followed by the 105th Regt. (2nd. Batt. The King's Own Yorkshire Light Infantry) who kept them for the next two seasons. The Norfolk Regiment kept a pack at Colchester barracks when stationed there in 1890, and in 1892 the pack were passed on to the Northamptonshire Regiment who took their place at Colchester when the Norfolks were posted abroad; on their return the Regiment was sent to the old East India Company Barracks at Warley near Brentwood where, by 1906, they became the possessors of a pack originally owned by the Welch Regiment who had hunted them in the Gravesend area. These fifteen couple of hounds were hunted around Brentwood twice a week for three seasons.

Surprisingly the next year saw two further packs in Essex, both civilian and nearer London: the Braxstead Park kennelled at Witham, which K.S.Gladstone began to hunt in the East Essex Foxhounds' country twice a week and continued right up to 1913, and the Wolverston which started off being kennelled at Woolston Hall, Chigwell on the edge of Essex Foxhounds' territory. The latter were the property firstly of Philip Savill, but subsequently Winifred Savill kept them going until 1940 by which time the country was on short commons because of the war, and with the fall of France England had to tighten its belt in earnest with no time for what were considered, regretfully, the non essentials of war. Phemie Angus's father, Dr. Thomas Cochrane Angus, used to whip in to the Wolverston prior to the 1939/45 War. He had been a RNAS pilot in the First War,

Banks Farm Harriers February 1935.
'Phemie Angus and sister' the earliest photo. (Phemie Angus Collection)

Wolverston Beagles 1935. Phemie's father whipped in. (Phemie Angus Collection)

transferring to the RFC and awarded a DFC; he flew a great lumbering Handley Page 0400 with 216 Squadron RFC and on release after the First War subsequently turned to science in medical research and took exercise with hounds in his spare time, whipping in until 1939.

By 1911 (according to B.G.E.Webster), The Riverdale Beagles had been formed by Lt.Col. W. Russell-Johnson CBE DSO and he hunted the Rochford Hundred, which includes Rayleigh, Rochford and Fambridge, for a season. As a serving officer he appears to have taken his hounds wherever he was posted but they were kennelled at Reed Hall, Colchester for a while and were apparently on loan in 1921 to the Garrison's officers. From there they hunted the Dengie Peninsular between the River Blackwater and the River Crouch, westward towards Chelmsford and Billericay. In 1923 hounds were sold to the Colchester Garrison, the country having been given up. The Colchester Garrison Beagles lasted until the outbreak of war, but there was a resurgence of Garrison beagling in 1956 when the Dundonald Beagles (Royal Artillery) returned to Colchester and reformed as the Colchester Garrison Beagles with their country within that of the Essex and Suffolk, and East Essex Foxhounds until 1994.

Bassett hounds had made their appearance in Essex in 1910, a pack having been founded as early as 1889 by Capt. Godfrey Heseltine and his brother Christopher, then becoming the Slane Bassett Hounds under Marquis Conyngham in 1903, and reverting to Godfrey Heseltine later, renamed the Walhampton Bassett Hounds, and kennelled at Billericay until 1915 when he moved to the Midlands. One of the whips had been a former Essex Union huntsman, Arthur Webster.

Wolverston unboxing. Huntsman & KH Arthur Threader arriving at a meet. (Phemie Angus Collection)

Some years after the Great War Mr. and Mrs. Davies living at Limbourne Park decided to form a pack, naturally enough called the Limbourne Park Beagles and despite the vicissitudes of the war years managed to survive until 1946. This became a very well known pack of 14 inch hounds that were in great demand as progenitors of later packs and established a much sought after line. There was also for a short while in 1940 a pack which did not reach the stud book known as the Bulphan Beagles, somewhat higher at the shoulder, formed by Byass Shepherd of Greystead House, Bulphan and kept at Margaretting. They were no longer in existence when the war ended.

In Essex in 1947 there was a greengrocer who had a flourishing business in Elm Park, William Knight (always known as Bill to his friends). He was born in Kent where his father farmed and he was steeped in country lore having kept the odd hound and hunted with a few friends around the family fields at Headcorn. At some time he had even ridden as an amateur in the Grand National. He was a good horseman and still rode daily in later life before his final retirement.

Someone walked into the shop whilst Bill was serving a customer and so Bill turned to him in due course to find out what he wanted. To his horror the fellow asked for his support for a Parliamentary bill to end hunting. Unfortunately for him he had come to the wrong man, Bill told him in no uncertain terms his feelings on this point and the chastened petitioner beat a hasty retreat. It still rankled in Bill's mind for some time after and gradually the plan formed in his mind to make a practical gesture against the people who wanted to end hunting. He decided to form his own pack of beagles: the Hornchurch Beagles.

The first hurdle was to find farmers who would give support and allow him to hunt their land: this he did. Next, to find hounds for the pack. He turned to

*Limbourne Park Beagles at Limbourne Park.
L to R: Jack Pertwee (whip), Mr Davies MH and
huntsman, Mrs. Davies, Allen KH and whip.
(Phemie Angus Collection)*

Frank Witherden who kept a few hounds, and from him he obtained some, ending up with a nucleus of 4½ couple, and then contacted others for a few more. The first season found Bill able to take the field with hounds and he hunted them with enjoyment, but disaster struck after only two days hunting when hounds in kennels went down with hard pad. Despite all Bill could do he had lost 9½ couple before the kennels were declared clear by the vet. Luckily he had saved some puppies which he was able to enter the following season with other hounds Frank Witherden brought out and for a time it was a trencher fed pack, kept individually by various people who brought them to the meet, though the hunting was excellent, and by the 1949/50 season he was able to record 36 days hunting and accounted for 5½ brace of hares. The whips were Jim Hocking, later Hon.Secretary of the Mid Essex, Jack Pertwee and Simon V.N.Casey, a contributor to The Shooting Times in later life. Over at Spurriers, Norton Heath, Capt.A.C.C.Dunford-Hawkins kept a few couple of hounds and he arranged with Bill Knight to hunt their hounds together. Bill and Tony Hawkins had a great regard for hounds in common and the joint venture prospered. For the next season hounds' tally was 7 brace, eclipsed in the 1951/2 season with 7½ brace. Tony Hawkins had retired from the Army and subsequently started a wine merchant's business based at Spurriers. One favoured hound 'Lancer' was largely given the run of the house and occasionally lifted his leg on the stacked wine bottles by way of choosing a good year for further inspection. Spurriers was a pleasantly mellowed red brick farmhouse with plenty of outbuildings which, among other uses, could be very convenient for kennelling hounds. Bill Knight and Tony Hawkins agreed for the start of the 1952/3 season to combine the packs under the name of the Mid-Essex Beagles and to kennel them at Spurriers. Bill moved to Ingatestone, which is much nearer to Spurriers, taking over as landlord of The Bell in the High Street where he was able to stable a horse in the garage, which he exercised daily after closing the bar at 2.30 p.m. In time his interest grew in greyhound coursing and he kept some greyhounds himself, but in later life when he was no longer mobile he would often be driven to a meet of the Mid Essex by his son to cast a critical eye on the pack, usually approvingly. He lived for over a century and saw many changes, but not the demise of hunting: he had made his point.

Bill Knight with hounds in the early days. (Phemie Angus Collection)

In 1959 Richard Hilder formed the North Essex Foot, their country widespread up to Sudbury and over to the Essex-Cambridgeshire border taking in Braintree, Witham, Dunmow and Thaxtead and partly adjoining the Mid-Essex and the Colchester Garrison. They also adjoined the de Burgh Bassets formed in the latter part of the 1959/60 season. Subsequently, towards the end of the 1975/6 season the de Burgh amalgamated with the then North Essex Foot Hunt Club and took over part of the North Essex country.

So, in due course the Mid-Essex found themselves with the North Essex Foot, ultimately the de Burgh and North Essex, on their north west flank, the Colchester Garrison to the north east and the West Lodge Harehounds to the west, the south and east boundaries being the Thames and the sea respectively.

Today Essex is criss-crossed by fast A roads and encroached on by the M25 and the M11. New towns, Harlow, Basildon and Woodham Ferrers have appeared, other older towns have mushroomed with housing development and the population has expanded greatly. In 1949 it was only a short time since the war had ended and Government restrictions were still in force on food and clothes rationing, fuel was scarce; the first Morris Minor with the split windscreen and a side valve engine was not yet on the market, and for the time being it would only be for export anyway. Dirty steam rolling stock in urgent need of replacement, worn out buses, taxis and the ubiquitous bicycle were the main means of transport. Lorries were ancient pre-war vehicles that could carry little so that the majority of goods were transported by the vast railway network and much of agriculture was still a mixture of old and new, though the war had increased the use of tractors and mechanical aids. Many men and women were

Phemie as huntsman. The earliest photo in which she carries the horn. (Phemie Angus Collection)

Brewers Arms, Bicknacre. From an old Christmas card (Clive Petchey Collection)

Bill Knight 12 Feb 1955. Behind the bar and awaiting with trepidation Renard's opinion of the beer. (Phemie Angus Collection)

still in H.M.Forces, the Cold War had started with the Berlin Airlift and the National Service Act 1948 had come into force on the 1st. January 1949.

The countryside was much as it had been during the war and to a great extent, apart from Ministry of Agriculture wartime requirements to improve food production, had changed very little from pre-war other than the building of airfields and Army camps. Some aerodromes were deserted already with skeleton staffs as caretakers, the farmers now beginning to hope for the return of the requisitioned land. RAF Hornchurch, the Sutton's Farm of the first World War, was no longer used for operational purposes, it had no concrete runways, and in the 1950s became an Air Crew Selection Unit where Ronnie Corbett of 'The Two Ronnies', the TV programme, served as a National Service officer; Boreham airfield, an American war-time medium bomber base, would be used as a racing circuit; Stapleford Tawney grass airfield, before the war used by Hillman for his air taxi service and flips for the public while he ran scheduled flights as well, in wartime a communications airfield, was to revert to civilian use. Willingale, another American bomber base, was never used again though one of the contenders for a third London airport later. North Weald aerodrome was revived for RAF Auxiliary Squadrons to use for modern jet fighters and Rochford, a Battle of Britain airfield going back to the First World War, became in time Southend Airport. Army camps if not retained would disappear more easily.

The bicycle was still a major means of transportation for short distances, or one might beg a lift if no bus was available, but with little traffic on the roads, even though they were in great need of repair, they were a pleasure to be on.

To have a pack of hounds and be able to take them over the plough not worrying too much about traffic on the bisecting country lanes was absolute luxury by comparison with present day problems. An old 10th Hussars' major, who in his younger days hunted with the Essex Union Foxhounds, was known to boast that they sometimes ran so near London they would toss up whether to go home or on to the Savoy for tea: when the Mid Essex was formed one could still hunt around Chigwell and down to the Thames.

There was some good country in Essex and although mainly arable one could find some very pleasant grassland here and there. Farmers had started to pull out hedgerows to enlarge fields: combines were getting bigger and more turning space was needed, and over a large area the increase in acreage under plough was much enlarged by the ripping out of hedges with a higher yield overall. The Essex Prairies were here to stay, so instead of small hedged fields in the pre-war style one saw vast acreages of plough uninterrupted by any hedge or trees and occasionally bisected by a drainage ditch. This became the norm for the Mid Essex, though the pack sometimes hunted fruit orchards at the request of the owners and up on the dykes near the coast where cattle vied with geese for the grassland, or over dairy farmland with its tightly hedged fields and cattle gently ever curious as to the goings on of the pack and the followers, but sheep were better left a field or two away, and goats best forgotten. Horses always took an interest, whether hunters, carthorses, or trained to the plough and galloped up and down the hedge for the best view, often if hounds were not speaking a good indication of the direction they had taken a field or two away out of sight.

When the pack was formed economically the country was just recovering from wartime curbs but the pound was still worth four dollars – not the 1.60 when it disbanded. Although there was little fluctuation in the purchasing power of the pound in the early days, nevertheless during the life of the Mid Essex money was to play an important part in its existence and, as will be seen, finances could swing overnight practically, and at one moment be comfortable and the next down almost to disaster level. Had it not been for the generosity of members, supporters and friends over the years the Mid Essex might not have lasted its half century – and yet it did. It was the changing face of Essex that really caused its demise. Urbanisation and roads were its downfall.

CHAPTER 2

Moving off
and Finding

The Mid Essex Beagles, as the hunt was registered with the Association of Masters of Harriers and Beagles (the governing body for hare hunting in the UK, founded in 1891), began life at Spurriers, the home of Capt. and Mrs. Tony Hawkins at Norton Heath between Ongar and Chelmsford. Arthur Whittaker became the paid kennel huntsman, and at the first meeting held at The Bell, Ingatestone, on the evening of Thursday, 10th September 1953, a committee of hunt subscribers and the joint masters, Bill Knight and Tony Hawkins, was formed.

David Baddeley was elected chairman, a post he was to hold for about 20 years. An old friend of the Angus family, David in his day had been a great rowing man to which the oars adorning his hallway gave testimony, having stroked for the Vesta Rowing Club at Putney, winning the Thames Cup at Henley in 1930 and the Silver Goblet in 1937, and during the war was a RNVR minesweeper flotilla commander in the Mediterranean theatre. His family business, Baddeley Brothers was well known in the City as producers of fine letterhead dies amongst other printing items. David himself was a gruff, sturdy dependable prop for any organisation, who did not suffer fools gladly yet gave a loyalty without reserve, his no-nonsense approach epitomised in his usual grace growled out at dinners, 'Good food, good wine. Thank God!'

Simon Casey became the first Secretary and Dick Richards, a dapper, sharp featured, moustachioed, Westminster Bank Manager in Chelmsford, was elected Treasurer, and a subscription of 3 guineas (£3.15) with a cap of 3s 6d (just over 17p) per day for casual followers was fixed.

The Mid Essex Beagles were in business, and despite trials and tribulations over the next fifty years they would become a well known pack and acquire a great reputation in the beagling world. Hounds would be bred and the distinct line maintained through generations of hounds as will be described later.

Uniform for those invited to wear it was a green hunting coat with dark blue velvet collar, black hard hunting cap, white breeches, green socks, and shoes to personal choice ranging from gym shoes, hocky boots or anything else both comfortable and suitable to run in. Whips with thongs attached were carried in addition. The hunt button was the badge of a rising hawk with wings inverted, grasping a sword at the carry in its right talons, perched upon a castellated base (see illustration). Evening dress was green tail coat with mustard facings and dark blue velvet collar.

The first Committee meeting was held at Spurriers on the 19th September and an enthusiastic committee decided to not only run a Christmas Draw but to fix the date for a Hunt Ball as well at the Heybridge Hotel, Ingatestone for the price of 35 shillings a single ticket, 3 guineas for a double (£1.75 & £3.15 respectively). Obviously the funds produced by both were a welcome addition. Further, in 1954 a draw, this time for the Derby, was arranged and also a hunt dance run jointly with the Eastern Counties Otter Hounds, (today the Eastern Counties Mink Hounds).

A hunt ball was an annual event for all hunts where the ladies wore their favourite gowns and the men their hunt tail coats or black tails if they had them, dinner jackets otherwise. It was a colourful sight and in the case of the Mid Essex beaglers or harriers green tail coats were intermingled on the dance floor with the red tail coats of foxhunters, and even one doctor resplendent in his kilt! A horn blowing competition, by tradition, was held later in the evening and the prize was usually a bottle of whisky. One year it was won by a whip's father who did not hunt but was egged on to try his luck – he had served in his early youth in the Royal Navy as a ship's bugler! A tombola was always a good money maker during the evening.

Not only that, the hunt put on its first puppy show in the summer at Spurriers. This in itself was not an easy thing to arrange. The two judges from other packs had to be invited, usually a Master and a huntsman, a ring fenced off with paling in which to exhibit hounds on the lawn at the side of the house, the

Hunt Button

grass mowed immaculately, chairs found, teas prepared, the bowler hat and long coat found for the kennel huntsman (and remember to provide discreet shovels to hand to clear up any droppings), and in the ring dogs and bitches to be kept separate. It was also the time when silver spoons were presented to puppy walkers, those who had taken one or more hounds into their care during the puppies' young days before entering, and cups awarded for the year to those who had walked, in the opinion of the judges, the best dog or best bitch. For the people involved this was a nerve taxing experience and much hard work went into it. Rain was the last thing wanted.

The committee even managed to fix the first farmers' dinner at the Kings Head, Ongar for which members were charged 12s. 6d. each, no doubt to cover the cost of a farmer as well for it was the traditional way to thank the farmers or landowners over whose land hounds had hunted during the season. The dinner, or supper, was a male only affair and wives definitely not invited. The members of the hunt were expected to buy the drinks for the guests as well as provide the meal and the farmers very much appreciated the evening; remember this was before the breathalyser!

Apart from having to arrange meets the Masters had to ensure that meet cards were sent out to members, the landowners over whose land the pack would be hunting, and all those who were casual followers or friendly to the hunt and wished to be kept in the picture. This could be quite an expense and so the committee decided that for non-members a charge would be made of 7s 6d (approximately 37p.) per season. It would give a welcome relief to funds and keep the treasurer happy.

In addition to his duties as Honorary Secretary Simon Casey also carried a whip with Jim Hocking and Phemie Angus. Jim was a foundry manager with the Ford Motor Company in Dagenham and Captain of Ford's rugby A team, a wiry Welshman who had the ability to puzzle out the line almost as well as a hound. His cheerful Welsh voice calling to hounds over the plough became part of the scene for many years. Phemie Angus, a young girl in her early twenties, lived with her parents both keen on hunting and was greatly encouraged by them. She whipped in with enthusiasm and together the whips gave a good account of themselves.

Before the formation of the Mid Essex and before the start of the 1952/3 season hounds had been taken up to Westmoreland on the fells and given a taste of hill country, far different from the deep plough of Essex but a foretaste of trips to Wales which were to become an annual event for many years.

With hounds all kennelled at Spurriers it became necessary to have appropriate transport and Tony Hawkins had a hound van built to his specification by a local motor company, something that regretfully could not be repeated out of hunt funds in subsequent years. It was a diesel van on a Trojan chassis and could carry 13 couple of hounds and 5 people, or 13 passengers. There is no record of the latter being carried after hounds had enjoyed the comforts! The Motor Company's advertisement for the vehicle shows a partition

Phemie with Jim Hocking (the late Frank H. Meads by permission of Jim Meads)

behind the driver and venetian shutters at the side windows with a form of hound lodge on which hounds could lie during the journey. Whatever happened to it is unknown for by 1959 another van had to be purchased secondhand and modified to carry hounds.

By 1955 Jim Hocking had taken over as Honorary Secretary from Simon Casey and hounds formally became the property of Tony Hawkins, who also took over as Master of the Essex Farmers Foxhounds until 1957. Hunting was reduced to two days a week instead of three and in future would meet on Wednesdays and Saturdays at 1130 am. During the 1955/6 season for the first time Phemie Angus officially took over the horn as amateur huntsman and carried it until the end of the 2003/4 season, without a break save for an extremely rare bout of sickness. Tony Hawkins took over the responsibility for the payment of the new kennelman, Bill Katt following in Arthur Whittaker's footsteps, at £2 per week. In

Spurriers 1956. Jack Pertwee leaning over to talk to Phemie in the old kennel run. (Author's Collection)

Meet 1956. The van is an interesting vehicle – possibly ex-Army. (Author's Collection)

that year hounds had been taken to the Honiton Hound Show meeting with some success. Funds must have been rather strained for the subscription was raised to 5 guineas (£5.25), the cap having been increased some time before to 5 shillings (25p).

The Mid Essex Beagles were beginning to make a name in the hunting world.

The country at this time was mainly arable – most being sticky glutinous plough during the start of the season, the tines having dug deep as was then fashionable, and it needed long legs to cover the ridges at any speed, whilst those with shorter legs heaved and struggled and it was obvious that a pair of hocky boots that could be dunked in a bucket of water had the advantage over tennis shoes, which might be sucked off in the struggle. There was not much grassland, which was so rare as to seem strange after miles of plough or kale. Sometimes there was a hill to make for to give a good view, but most of the time the only vantage point over the flatter parts of the land was a welcome farm gate to stand or sit on. Where woodland intervened, and hounds might be lost to view temporarily if the hare made for cover, it was all ears acock to hear the peal of hound music deflected by the trees as they picked up the scent once more after a short check.

Eric Dix joined Jim Hocking as joint secretary in 1957. Eric was a larger than life figure, always elegantly attired in hacking coat, white stock and breeches and able to deal with the field with skill and the utmost tact, the younger members of the field, being greatly impressed by his turnout and good manners, trying to emulate him which was no bad thing. In the same year Tony Hawkins gave up his mastership of the Essex Farmers and became Master of the Essex Union

Pub at Nine Ashes, Blackmore. Possibly Wheatsheaf. (Colin Miller Collection)

RAF Hornchurch Meet 1959. Morning after the Hunt Ball in the Officers' Mess (Author's Collection)

Hornchurch aerodrome, scene of many a "dog-fight" during the Battle of Britain, gave way to another chase on Saturday. The Essex Beagles, yelping hounds and all, led a hare hunt from the aerodrome across the surrounding countryside. This is the first time the Essex Beagles have visited Hornchurch.

Foxhounds. Obviously, especially on Saturdays, foxhounds claimed his attention more than the beagles.

When Eric Dix moved away in 1959 to Hertfordshire Colin Miller took his place as joint Honorary Secretary. Colin had joined the Mid Essex when he was a young bachelor on the strength of Fords Agricultural Division at Boreham Hall near Chelmsford. He invested in an early model Landrover to drive himself and friends to meets. At his last meet with the Mid Essex at the Cuckoo, Radley Green, Eric was determined to make it a memorable occasion and after hounds moved off he and Jim Hocking tarried in the bar for a while to reminisce. This became rather thirsty work and somewhat time consuming so when they eventually emerged, manfully supporting each other, no hounds were in site and not a sound of them could be heard. Immediately they let out a holler in unison and stood waiting patiently for hounds to give tongue. Nothing happened, so off they went cheerfully arm in arm into the distance, ever hopeful of finding hounds, the field and Phemie. The writer met up once again with Eric Dix and his wife in the 1990s – they lived in an old rectory just a couple of miles away, and for some years until his death we would meet at the Fakenham Races where Eric's judicious eye for a horse in the paddock was rarely miscast, as the bookies ruefully admitted.

By this time the committee had to think about replacing the hound van. A new one was out of the question on the funds available and it was decided to buy a secondhand van but to replace the engine with a new or reconditioned one, the usual practise at the time as the engines wore out before the chassis and bodywork. In the same year Tony Hawkins's wife, Esther, became Joint Master so that there was always at least one Master in the field at each subsequent meet, especially necessary when Tony was with the foxhounds though he tried to join the beaglers if foxhounds blew for home early in the day, his red coat adding some colour to the scene. In that year, too, a joint meet was arranged with the Sproughton Foot though no record exists of how it went, or whether it was in their country for they hunted south of Ipswich and beyond the River Stour which was the northern boundary of the Colchester Garrison Beagles. Meet fixtures were advertised for the first time in Southend on Sea newspapers to encourage more to follow. Yet again hounds were shewn at the Aldershot, Peterborough and Harrogate Hound Shows.

The next year Roy Lawrence became first whip for the 1960/61 season and Peter Hopton and Tim Bailey, grandson of Warren Squier, were appointed 2nd joint whips. Peter Hopton was well known in the City as a Marine Assessor. This did sometimes interfere with his beagling for he certainly lived a varied life dashing hither and thither all over the world, perhaps to Alexandria to examine a stinking cargo of skins that had self ignited on board ship: Roy worked in London, but had more Saturdays available. A friendship between Roy and Peter

Opening meet at Spurriers 1960 (Colin Miller Collection)

Opening Meet at Spurriers 1960 (Colin Miller Collection)

Orsett 1960 In uniform, L. to R. Roy Lawrence, Phemie, Colin Miller and Peter Hopton. (Colin Miller Collection)

grew up in the beagling field and they did much work around the kennels and exercising hounds at weekends in the early hours of the morning, often giving a whoop outside the closed curtains of the writer, then living in Stondon Massey, if they thought he should be up and about! Dick Richards acquired a Miss Lovell to be joint Treasurer. The kennelman had a pleasant surprise, for the committee made sure that the cap at the last meet of the season went to him.

When the season had finished the subscription was raised to 7 guineas (£7.35), though there was no change to the 5/- cap, and the members took over the responsibility for the kennelman's wages.

Dick Richards found himself sole Treasurer again by 1962 and with even greater problems, for yet another hound van had to be bought and the Farmers' Dinner, held at the Golden Fleece, Chelmsford had to be paid for as the moneys from the sale of tickets to members never covered the cost, and hunt funds always had to subsidise it annually. Yet it was worth while for it was a small recognition

Boreham Hall 26 November 1961Phemie with Esther Hawkins behind. (Colin Miller Collection)

Phemie at Boreham Hall 26 November 1961 (Colin Miller Collection)

of the help, co-operation and free use of their land the farmers gave each year without stint.

During this period the meets had settled down to a routine during the season, the opening meet being at Spurriers, and a few early morning meets beforehand, with most meets before the New Year to the east of the country in the main: after that more nearer Chelmsford and south. The meet on the first Saturday in the New Year in 1965 appears to have taken place at Thrift House, Chigwell Row, David Baddeley's house – about the nearest venue to London! The Rabbits, Stapleford Abbotts was still a favourite and The Cricketers, Danbury, even for the Farmers' Supper, was still a regular on the meet card. (No doubt some will remember there, after dinner, an old entertainer appeared dressed in a farm smock going under the name of 'Jan Stewer' to tell wonderful country stories in a broad accent.) In the south one could still meet at The Harrow, Bulphan, and the Dog and Partridge at Orsett, or far over to the east at Canewdon, the favourite of witches, and among the ancient Red Hills of the salt makers of Essex.

After 12 years as kennelman Bill Katt moved on and his place was taken in 1965 by Clive Knott who lived in at Spurriers and his wage of £7 per week was split between the Masters and the members. His duties were to include whipping in and driving the hound van.

Jim Hocking resigned as joint Secretary after 10 years and Colin's wife, Terry, took his place. Phemie had one of her rare days off unwell one Saturday meet at the Cats, Woodham Walter so Jim carried the horn, much to his delight,

The Queen, Purley. 1965 (Clive Petchey Collection)

and delivered a fine day's hunting as a result. Much later, when Phemie had her only other day off Derek Gardener hunted hounds at The Ship Stock. Another joint meet with the Sproughton took place on the 19th February 1966 at the George, Hintlesham. Other meets, among many, were held at the Boar's Head, Herongate; the Barge, Battlesbridge; the Cats, Woodham Walter over farmland belonging to John Speakman, R.J.Carter, B. Ratcliff, C.Warner and I. Fowles; and the Cherry Tree, Rochford, whilst tea at the Compasses, West Hanningfield, and the Pig & Whistle in Chignal Smealy were memorable events. During March hounds met at the Ferry Boat, North Fambridge and the Sportsmans Arms, Nounsley by way of a change. During the 1966/7 season most of the meets were the old favourites with the addition of Great Malgraves at Horndon on the Hill; Sutton Hall, Rochford; Beauchamps, Shopland, and New Hall, Boreham (by kind

Wheatsheaf 1966
Numbered from left: 4 Derick Carlisle, 6 Capt.Tony Hawkins MH, 11 Phemie Angus (huntsman),
12 Esta Hawkins MH, 13 David Baddeley (chairman), 14 Clive Nott (kennelman)
(Colin Miller Collection)

Beagles at the Cats

MAKING a return visit to The Cats, Woodham Walter, on Saturday, were the Mid-Essex Beagles. The beagles visited The Cats in February towards the end of the 1964 to 1965 season, but Saturday's visit was only about the third of the new season.

The Cats was the beagles headquarters for the day, but they did not manage to catch any hares. A spokesman explained that the ground was not in a good enough condition for the beagles to find a scent because of the weather.

The Cats, Woodham Walter. Clive Nott and Esther Hawkins in uniform, Betty Bolingbroke extreme right. (Clive Petchey Collection)

permission of the Reverend Mother) was an unexpected pleasure with girls and nuns from the school joining in. Further west Murrells Farm, Stamford Rivers was fixed for a Wednesday meet. Sutton Hall was almost next door to Southend Airport, once a First World War flying field, later used by Hillman for connecting flights to the continent, a Second World War airfield, and home of the unfortunate Channel Airways in the '60s. It could be rather noisy, but neither hounds nor hare seemed put out.

By 1967 Clive Knott left and he was replaced by Vic Ramsey who agreed to do two hours a day as kennelman for £5 10s (£5.50) per week paid by the committee, but matters were about to take a significant turn for Tony and Esther Hawkins decided to move to Wales. With both joint Masters about to leave the country not only was the hunt in danger of possibly folding up, the question of where hounds would be kennelled also arose if the hunt were to continue.

CHAPTER 3

The Check

There was a lot of heart searching and discussion when it became known that the Joint Masters were leaving Essex. Phemie Angus had hunted the pack for twelve years, knew each hound by name, was steeped in the lore of hunting and knew the country and the landowners, and so an agreement was reached whereby Phemie was to become Joint Master and the pack formally handed over by Tony Hawkins to her care whilst he remained absentee joint master, but he resigned his joint mastership of the Essex Union Foxhounds.

A special Meeting (presumably of the Committee though unclear from the minutes) was held on the 20th July 1967 at Bernard Henderson's home at which possible kennelling at a building in Highwood was considered but dropped as derelict, in need of much work, and it could not be made ready under 6 to 9 months. However, a new home for hounds had yet to be found. At Little Totham, several miles north east of Maldon were the kennels of the Eastern Counties Otterhounds. This pack had started in 1898 as the Essex Otterhounds and changed its name about 1909. Already both packs were on easy terms for some years before they had held a joint dance as already mentioned in Chapter One. Their distinctive blue coats with red collars, white breeches and red stockings were often to be seen hunting the rivers in East Anglia for otter with their thick coated, shaggy looking hounds . Mr H Townsend and Mrs M Hale were the joint Masters of the Otterhounds at the time and Bob Street was kennelman looking after about 23 couple of hounds. Nevertheless there was plenty of spare space at the otterhounds' kennels and a satisfactory arrangement was made for the Mid Essex hounds to board there as well, with Bob Street to look after both packs in kennels. Typical farm buildings were the core of the set up, certainly there seemed to be no lack of bibles to feed hounds, and exercising was no problem.

An Extraordinary Meeting attended by about 30 members was held on the 23rd August at the Bull, Blackmore. Colin Miller could not attend so Bernard

Henderson took the minutes, recorded in a lively fashion by him. The draft agreement was read out and subject to getting a reduction in rent thought to be too high, and better security of tenure, it was accepted. The future running cost of the pack would now be about £1,000 per annum as rent and light now had to be paid for, though David Baddeley did say that the pack would be reduced to 20 couple, at which point Phemie Angus added 'plus a few whelps, as agreed with Maureen' (Maureen Hale, one of the ECOH Joint Masters) – she had to think about the future. Subscriptions had to be increased to cover the rent for the new kennels, a factor not present in the accounts whilst at Spurriers, and the new membership figure suggested was 10 guineas (£10.50), over three times the original 1953 subscription! Although this increase was proposed and seconded Derick Carlisle pointed out that this could not be approved at an Extraordinary Meeting and would have to wait for the AGM on the 13th September. Several opposed the increase; to cap it, and more to the point, Jim Hocking, to everyone's delight, remarked that the beer they were drinking was foul, whilst Clive Petchey coming back to earth pointed out the 10 guineas was too much for young members and it was agreed that this was all right for those over 25, but under that age 7 guineas (£7.35) was reasonable. There was some argument between the Treasurer and Derick Carlisle on the cash merits of the draw, the Treasurer having given his opinion that the Hunt Ball and the Draw were 'pot luck'; Derick Carlisle hotly contested this, reckoning that the draws would bring in at least £250 by the end of the week after the Grand National. Several other ideas were put up and thrown out, including the Author's suggestion of a Supporters' Club, a post point-to-point ball, and Associate Membership – but at least people began to get the message that more cash must be found.

It was a greatly relieved committee who accepted the terms and conditions of joint occupancy. The idea of the alternate Highwood site was finally dropped. At the AGM the membership subscription was increased to the Extraordinary Meeting figures with the addition of new members paying 7 guineas for the first two seasons and a family subscription of 12 guineas (£12.60) minimum. Peter Hopton, over the course of the last few seasons, had been collecting caps at meets with immense success and now he had the additional job of tactfully asking those who had been capped three times in a season to become subscribers. The Hunt Club had been revived at last and subscription for membership fixed at 10 guineas. Jim Hocking found himself detailed off to prepare an article on the Hunt for the *Essex Countryside* magazine. Terry Miller had reluctantly relinquished her joint secretaryship due to illness and Colin soldiered on by himself as Secretary.

Hounds moved into their new quarters on 11th September 1967. Esther Hawkins gave up her joint mastership and her husband became joint master with Phemie Angus. Tony Hawkins on moving, by retaining his position as joint master in the Mid Essex, gave continuity to what might have been a traumatic changeover period in the hunt's history. Unfortunately, there was a period of three months when no hunting was possible due to Foot & Mouth restrictions, though this did not stop Phemie Angus afterwards from making a tally of 23½ brace in twenty days hunting. The Cross Keys at Roxwell, The Plough & Sail, East Hanningfield, Hutton Church, Mucking Hall at Barling Marsh were all visited during the remains of the season with the closing meet at the Ship, Stock (more often a New Year's meet).

The 1967/8 season was mixed in that good results were obtained from the subscriptions, Hunt Ball and draws, though as a result of meets cancelled due to foot and mouth caps were down. £150 was put on deposit towards a new hound van. Jim Hocking had been organising meets for some time. The Committee were warned that Bob Street would be leaving the ECOH kennels at Christmas and the Otterhounds would have to find a replacement. Some prizes had been taken by hounds at Peterborough though competition was fierce.

As previously mentioned, for some years it had been a tradition for a nucleus of members to take hounds to Wales for a week and hunt them there before the start of the season in Essex. The accommodation found at The Lion Royal, Rhayader, was so much to everyone's liking that it developed into an annual treat for those who could afford the time to spare, and year after year the Welsh hills rang to the cry of the beagles and after dusk to the jollities of the followers. Colin Miller well remembers having to take hounds up to the Afonwy foxhound kennels and feed and bed them down in straw after a strenuous day's hunting, only to find returning to the hotel tired and dishevilled and looking forward to a bath that the 'non-working' members had taken all the hot water. Another time he was pleasantly surprised to see several local farm youths turning out to follow hounds, though disappointed to find their real interest was in following up the hills the shapely bottom of one of the young girl beaglers and their interest did not stretch to hounds at all.

According to Clive Petchey hounds were usually taken to Rhayader a couple of days before the first meet so that they could be introduced to free running sheep. The Afonwy kennels were at a lonely, brick built barn deep in the Elan Valley and the Master was Elwyn Collard, son of the hotel landlord, Bill Collard; Elwyn and his wife, Mary, took over running the hotel later on when his parents retired. Some of the bedrooms in those days only had linoleum on the floors, cold to the feet when hoisting stiff bodies out of bed in the morning but the shock produced a wide awake beagler seconds later. The Saturday meet was the opener, about ten Mid Essex beaglers plus the Hawkins with Phemie Angus to hunt the pack would turn out together with a crowd of local farmers and shepherds. The intention was to educate hounds for the coming season by hunting every other day and get them fit for the heavy clay of Essex; but not only that, between hunting days, various excursions were made and the Essex beaglers were also able to enjoy the mountains, hills, valleys, lakes and woodland with the occasional moorland in a variety of weather; even pony trekking, though Clive Petchey found this somewhat disconcerting as he gradually slipped off when he discovered his pony's girth had been loosened by one of the party. Sometimes the beaglers hunted with other packs, such as the Glyn Cellyn Beagles from Builth

Wells of whom the Masters were Lt. Col. A.S. Jervis MBE and his wife. Apart from The Lion Royal, in subsequent years the Elan Valley Hotel, a place by the Wye River bridge, the Red Lion at Llandinum, and the Old Vicarage at Llangurig became the beaglers temporary homes.

The Lion Royal had a dimly lit back bar usually frequented by farmers and shepherds, especially after profitable sheep and cattle days in the market and the beaglers made merry there, even re-enacting a bull fight with a pair of bull's horns, no doubt temporarily borrowed from the bar wall. Sometimes they went to listen to the local male voice choir rehearsing in another pub and afterwards encouraged them to sing more after lubricating them in the bar.

Geoff Dignum enjoyed the Welsh trips. Apparently hounds were kennelled at one time at the Bailey Walter, the home of Tony and Esther Hawkins, and Phemie had come over to the Lion Royal to roust out the Mid Essex members for a meet at Llangurig. In her haste she left her hunting cap at the hotel and only discovered her loss on arrival at the meet where Oakley Foot beaglers were waiting. She decided to start capless and Geoff went back to recover it. All the way to Rhayader he drove, collected the cap and retraced his steps. By the time he reached the meet Phemie was away over an adjacent hill with hounds, when Geoff arrived on the ridge Phemie was down into the next valley, so down the hill Geoff careered at breakneck speed only to see Phemie going fleet footed up the next hill. Somewhat out of puff he was finding all this very exasperating, but hounds checked and at last a breathless figure waving a cap was up with the huntsman.

However, to everyone's regret hounds managed only three days in Wales in 1968 and that was really the end of hounds' annual holiday, for interest had tailed off. Only twice were they to venture out of Essex in the future and that was by invitation in the Trinity Foot Country and a visit to Norfolk by invitation of the Norfolk Beagles Hunt Club. Nevertheless the Petcheys and some other beaglers from Essex still make the pilgrimage to Wales in the autumn when they can.

The Farmers' Supper was held at the Halfway House Restaurant on the A127 in April 1968. This was owned by one of the Beaglers, Charles Farman, who farmed the land opposite. He later moved to Scarning and still found time to come down to hunt with the Mid Essex. A joint Terrier and Puppy Show was held with the Otterhounds at their kennels in the following June. Bill Knight had started hunting in 1947 and so a 21st Anniversary Dinner was held on 15th November 1968 at Chelmsford.

It was this year that Julia Asplin, the daughter of a local solicitor, joined Peter Hopton as joint Second Whip and Roy Lawrence continued as First Whip. Phemie Angus did not mind carrying the horn as well as exercising the authority and performing the duties of Master, for in fact Tony Hawkins was down in Wales most of the time. Nevertheless it was very difficult for Phemie to do all this, and draw up the meet card with its attendant necessary liaison with farmers and landowners to ensure no one was forgotten and all consents to hounds crossing land had been given. A meet was held in December at Rookwood Hall, Abbess

Phemie and Julia with hounds (Phemie Angus Collection – Photo by Stuart Turner)

The Ship, Stock. Popular as a Boxing Day meet for the crowd who came to wear off the Christmas Day lethargy. (Author's Photo)

Roding, the home of Mr. and Mrs. C. Rowe and another in February 1969 at the Bell, Tolleshunt Major with the permission of the Masters of the Colchester Garrison Beagles who hunted that part of the country.

During 1969 Derick Carlisle became joint secretary and responsible for arranging meets. This was a shrewd division of labour as Derick was a meticulous keeper of records and his maps and details, always up to date, of meets and the landowners affected, with individual notes on each one where necessary (for some could be a little cantankerous on occasion) were of inestimable value to his successors. Meets were fixed and cards went out – the whole like a military operation. This freed Phemie to spend more time with her beloved hounds and a chance to concentrate on the building up of a fine pack and to hunt them to the full. The result was a success. Derick had a direct approach to farmers and landowners which they appreciated and what was more, if they said hounds should not go in specific fields then Derick made sure their wishes were obeyed.

In April of that year the Committee were shewing concern at the condition of hounds in kennels and an adverse veterinary report had been obtained suggesting vaccination for all hounds as a remedy. It was felt hounds were not being looked after properly at the ECOH kennels and there was a certain amount of bad feeling between the hunts resulting, though after a change of Masters in the ECOH better relationships had resulted later on from a meeting between them and David Baddeley. However it was felt that alternative kennelling should be considered.

Phemie Angus had hunted with a season's tally of 23 brace and having taken $2^1/_2$ couple to Peterborough came away from the Show with 1st prize for Unentered Dog. A creditable feat. At the AGM Betty Bolingbroke received a commendation from Phemie for her care of the bitch 'Brevity', and her litter. The Welsh visit was cancelled. Dick Richards had been in touch with the North Essex Foot and it was hoped to hunt within the Dengie Hundred and further into the Rodings. Subsequently, although the Association Registrar became involved later, no further progress was made.

'Gangway' 1969 at the Peterborough Hound Show (Phemie Angus Collection – Frank H. Meads photo by permission of Jim Meads)

'Gangway'. 1969 A unique photo taken by Frank H. Meads' friend, of Phemie with hound being photographed by Frank for a magazine (Phemie Angus Collection by permission of Jim Meads)

Peterborough Hound Show. Until 1969 the MEB had some successful attendances. (Author's Photo)

Yet another hound van had to be found on the secondhand market. It is vaguely remembered as an Electricity Board van, more like a small pantechnicon big enough to carry poles and other equipment and even repainting did nothing to hide its origins. Doubtless fine for carting carcasses to feed hounds, though the fuel used by modern standards was horrific, and repairs were expensive when weighed against the value of the van.

Much to everyone's regret Jim Hocking retired from the Ford Motor Company and moved back to his native Wales in 1970. This left a gap in the continuity from the earlier days of the hunt for Jim had been there at the start. Dapper in appearance, his cheerful Welsh voice and impish grin were greatly missed. He dearly loved a morning's outing with terriers down a fox's earth if someone wanted to move Renard on from slaughtering hens. Also his knowledge of hound lore made him a useful asset to any hunt and he had done good work for the pack in his time in Essex.

The year had not been as good as previous ones; 11 days hunting having been lost and the tally down to 17 brace. Kennel problems were blamed. At Peterborough only a 4th and 5th prize had been taken. Phemie wanted to improve the pack's quality and so she arranged for some hounds to be drafted in: 1½ couple from the Newcastle & District Beagles, 1½ couple from the Aldershot Beagles , and one couple from the Trinity Foot Beagles. Hounds met at the Nags Head, Moreton early in December – this was a good venue for Richard Shweir's Nether Hall and its surrounding land: and on the 30th January 1971 there was a meet at East Hanningfield Hall, by invitation of Mr. Denis F.E. Benson when the cap was taken for the Royal Agricultural Benevolent Institute (known fondly to all as 'the Rabbi').

For the 1971/2 season the subscriptions were the highest ever though the kennel costs were rocketing and the Committee gloomily anticipated a demand for increased rent. Sure enough, by May 1971 the ECOH Masters wanted to increase the rent from £650 to £800. It was felt unjustified and the Committee decided that the continuation of kennelling there would be short term only and a further long term location was an urgent necessity. At the AGM in the County Hotel, Chelmsford another stalwart, David Baddeley, retired after chairing the hunt for 18 years. His place was taken by Frank Fitzwilliams. Dick Richards also retired that year having served as Treasurer for the same length of time as David

New Hall, originally built by Henry VIII after 1518, but subsequently a well known girls' school run by an order of nuns. (Phemie Angus Collection)

Baddeley had been Chairman. In the previous year Julia Asplin had been appointed joint treasurer with him and carried on alone for the time being. Frank Fitzwilliam, by profession an accountant, had made his name by resurrecting Achille Serre the well known cleaning company which had fallen on hard times, seizing it by the scruff of the neck and as chairman thrusting it into the limelight as a remodelled and successful company. He lived in Old Harlow and had a large family of his own, as well as numerous foster children. Very well liked and respected by all who came into contact with him he made an admirable replacement chairman. One evening he telephoned the writer and asked him to become the new treasurer. Who could refuse him? Julia became joint secretary with Colin Miller. A visit to Northumbria with hounds in 1972 was mooted.

Straightaway a problem arose concerning the hound van, or rather the lack of one. The old one had to be 'put down' and no substitute was in sight. As it was, one hoped a temporary measure, the Otterhounds' van was rented. The committee raised the subscription to £15 and the cap to 50p. However, the following year Bernard Henderson, a useful member with wide contacts, arranged the purchase of a van from the Essex County Council, it being 'surplus to requirement'. This resolved the difficulty for some time to come and was held on loan. During 1971 the Committee had to contend with the kennelling costs coupled with the lack of appropriate properties for future kennelling. A rearguard action was fought to contain the Little Totham increases. The Treasurer forecast that the year would end with a deficit of £190 on current shewing. A possible property near Cooksmill Green was investigated without success. Yet again the Hunt Club was to be revived.

Presentation to Joan Carlisle at The Cats Woodham Walter

L. to R.: Derek Gardiner (KH), Phemie Angus MH, David Baddeley, Joan Carlisle, Frank Fitzwilliam (Chairman), Derick Carlisle (Joint Secretary, Meets), Peter Hopton, (Whip), Colin Miller (Joint Secretary) Hounds digging up newly planted bulbs and Derick Carlisle had to appease the publican by purchasing a sack of bulbs to replace hounds' efforts. (the late Stuart Turner Collection)

Moving off from The Cats. (Author's Collection. Photo by Stuart Turner)

By January 1972 Derick Carlisle, as Meet Secretary was able to report progress in establishing new country, in particular within the Easters. Phemie Angus was still worried about the quality of the hounds. The Farmers' Supper was held at The County Hotel, Chelmsford in October 1972, not really the best venue. However the committee had to consider cost. (The previous year it had been at Bolingbroke & Wenley's Restaurant kindly arranged by Betty Bolingbroke, a strong supporter of the hunt, and one farmer mistakenly had brought his wife. Never had a lady, not even Phemie, attended a Farmer's Supper in the past and this was going to be no exception – she was bundled back to her car with apologies, a bunch of flowers and a box of chocolates!). Bernard Henderson arranged an evening at the Romford Greyhound Stadium for

Bernard Henderson in his famous voluminous breeches. (Author's Photo)

Clive Petchey with Phemie. (Author's Photo)

Committee members and wives which was hilarious, Tony Kidd shewing an uncanny knack for picking the winners. Dinner was served on the glassed in terrace, with the unnerving plunging into darkness of the tables every time a race started. It certainly concentrated the gaze if not the gastric juices.

A new agreement with the ECOH was finally approved at an Emergency Committee Meeting in May; even so, Phemie Angus said it would be a possibility to kennel hounds at her home. In October the Treasurer was feeling happier reporting to the AGM that caps, Hunt Ball profit, Draw, and Farmers' Supper were up: so too, were the van expenses and, of course, the rent, but there was even a small balance. It was decided not to increase the subscription. Phemie Angus confirmed the tally was 30 brace in 43 days' hunting with 2 days lost. She listed the problems: a shrinking country, busier roads and the difficult location of Office Farm for herself and her helpers, and not enough puppy walkers. Derick Carlisle was struggling with the accession of more space within the Essex Hunt country, but unfortunately an elderly Master was proving difficult to convince that the beagles should be allowed there. Derick hoped that there might be some meets in the west part of the Colchester Garrison Country.

The opening meet was at the White Hart, Margaretting Tye and in February 1973 hounds met at The Compasses in Holbrook, Suffolk by invitation of Sproughton Foot Beagles – the rest of the meets were at old favourites, including what had become the annual visit to David Baddeley's house at Chigwell Row – still the nearest meet to London.

1973 was a momentous year for the beaglers. Julia Asplin's wedding to Dr. Ian Porter, a local GP, was the event on the beaglers' calendar, for many were invited and turned up to the church service and reception. It was fine weather

Charles Farnham with John Schneidau, Clive Petchey, Julia and Ian Porter. (Clive Petchey Collection)

and many a beagler bedecked himself in morning suit instead of plus twos and hockey boots. Ian, luckily, was interested in hounds too. Frank Fitzwilliam attended the ECOH AGM and was satisfied that they would be continuing, but Phemie Angus still wanted improvements in kennel conditions. For the first time a Farmers' Supper was envisaged at Margaretting Village Hall with lady members providing the food which would reduce costs and at the same time ensure a good meal. The Hunt Ball was to be at the Heybridge Restaurant run by a new ladies committee. It was suggested that the Mid Essex country should be re-registered. The AGM was held in June and Phemie Angus mentioned that, despite difficult weather in the first half of the season, hounds had accounted for 20 brace in 37 days and in particular good days were seen at Rochford and Rettendon. The plea went out for puppy walkers for the two litters whelped. There was talk of visits to Norfolk arranged by Charles Farnham. Unfortunately, when the time for this came Phemie found it impossible because of various traumas with respect to kennelling.

By December, between them Phemie Angus and Derick Carlisle had successfully negotiated the opening up of more Essex Foxhounds country so that on the 8th December the meet was at The Fox, Mashbury for the first time and there was an invitation meet at the Three Horseshoes, Bannister Green, with one also by invitation at Delvyn's, Guestingthorpe. In addition two further invitations were obtained to the Plough, Radwinter and the Plough, White Notley, both towards the end of the season. These were the results of negotiations mentioned later.

The Fox, Mashbury, 30 March 1974 One of the most enjoyable meets with a magnificent tea to end the day's hunting (Phemie Angus Collection)

At the kennels Derek Gardiner had given notice to the ECOH that he would be leaving on !st May 1974. This was bad news. The first physical steps to obtain planning permission for kennels at Clavering took place on the 13th December and Strutt & Parker were instructed to apply for planning consent. Just before this ECOH had served notice on the Mid Essex to terminate the sharing arrangement on the following 25th March – in fact, little more than three months notice.

For the adjacent North Essex Foot there was a hesitant period in their fortunes. Their original Master, Richard Hilder, and owner of the hounds had started the pack in 1959 and carried the horn himself. Now he had had enough and wished to give up. There was much discussion as to whether part of the North Essex Foot country could be acquired and even some talk of amalgamation, though in effect for the Mid Essex this was the last thing it wanted in view of the problems over kennelling which took priority: it was neither the time nor the place to think of expansion either way. At one point there was even talk of North Essex hounds being taken over as a schoolboys' pack at Felsted School, Richard's Joint Master, Maj. Michael Mann MC, being a master there. However nothing came of this and the North Essex became a hunt club retaining the country until it was taken over by the de Burgh Basset hounds in 1976 and the name changed to the de Burgh and North Essex Harehounds.

There had been close co-operation between Tony Peel, joint Master of the North Essex, and the Committee of the Mid Essex during December and at a further meeting in January 1974 when Tony Peel was joined by his Joint Master, Michael Mann. The result was an arrangement whereby, for the rest of the 1973/4

Hounds in Kennels. (Phemie Angus Collection)

Phemie and Roy Lawrence (Author's Photo)

season the Mid Essex could hunt by invitation in the North Essex country on one Saturday and one Wednesday per month if North Essex hounds were continuing to hunt: two Saturdays and two Wednesdays per month if hounds were no longer kept by the North Essex.

CHAPTER 4

Casting Afresh – The Scent Regained – A New Beginning

The meeting in the Local Council at which the planning application for kennels at Clavering would be considered was in March 1974; the following month hounds were due to leave the Little Totham kennels. Temporary accommodation had been arranged with the Trinity Foot Beagles, the well known Cambridge college pack which can trace its history back to 1862, at their kennels in Barton, Cambridgeshire built in 1930. This was quite a way from the Mid Essex country but the new M11 could be useful, it might increase the petrol consumption of the hound van by longer journeys and the Canewdon or Rochford meets were quite a distance, but it was in reasonable reach for Phemie Angus from Clavering and nearer for her than Little Totham.

In Trumpington, at a well known hostelry, Phemie Angus, Frank Fitzwilliam and the author met for lunch with Charlie Barclay, Master of the Puckeridge and one of the Trustees of the Trinity Foot Beagles. Charlie Barclay, like many of his relations before him, had been a joint Master of the Trinity Foot at the advent of War and kept up his interest in the pack. The object of the luncheon was to hammer out any difficulties that could be foreseen and to set down the terms and conditions of sharing kennels. To everyone's relief the whole meeting went very well for Frank Fitzwilliam was a master of negotiation and he smoothed the way to an amicable arrangement very quickly. The Mid Essex contingent were taken over to inspect the kennels and met Jack Poile, the kennelman, and his wife and were entertained to tea by them. Jack was getting on in years and not quite so nimble by then, but still one of the best that could be found. They were a delightful couple and it was obvious that Jack ran a fine kennel. Hounds looked in good condition and the buildings and yard were well kept. Phemie was happy to let her hounds board there, and Frank too. The terms were fair and a great sense of relief was felt on the journey back.

Hounds transferred to Jack Poile's care and all was well. Funds were tight. Another second-hand van had to be bought so the committee came up with the idea of charging a 15p cap to subscribers which later on was increased to £1. To ease the long haul which the hound van had to make between meets and kennels it was decided to have a list of volunteers to drive the van on a rota basis. Certainly the opening of the M 11 helped for as yet it was hardly used. As the North Essex Foot were more or less in limbo as far as actively hunting their country was concerned some meets were arranged for the Mid Essex up there. This provided a great deal of interest.

Betty Bolingbroke and Eileen Hopton had produced a good Hunt Ball profit and the Farmers' Supper at Roxwell Village Hall was slightly profitable, whilst Julia Porter had run the Grand National Draw very successfully. Derek Gardiner, the kennel huntsman at the Little Totham kennels, had decided to move on and whip in to a Yorkshire pack of foxhounds and he was presented with a whip at the Farmers' Supper. He had enjoyed a good relationship with the Mid Essex and in later years everyone was pleased to hear he had become a Master of Foxhounds. Julia decided to give up whipping in. Phemie Angus, despite the difficult times the hunt was going through in the season, still managed a creditable 25 brace in 35 days. She pleaded for puppy walkers and it was obvious she was going to miss Julia's help.

By the July Committee meeting there was still no sign of planning consent for the new kennels. There had been an objection early on and it seemed there might now be a decision at the end of July. Derick Carlisle had applied to the Association Registrar with the consent of the Masters of the North Essex for registration of part of their country to be incorporated in the Mid Essex country and the result was awaited. The North Essex were offering 20 meets in their country for the 1974/5 season. The following month the Committee heard the planning authority had turned down the plans for the new kennels. It was decided to appeal by written representation, which was cheaper than a public hearing. Phemie was prepared to carry on with hounds kennelled at Cambridge for one more season. Another van was to be purchased with a loan from the bank. This was a second hand 1972 Ford Transit which needed some alterations

The ventilation grill put in the back door of the van. An absolute must. (Clive Petchey Collection)

The Compasses, Littley Green (Author's Photo)

Roddy Edwards and Christopher Latham in conference at the Compasses, Littley Green (Author's Photo)

Sonny Davey waiting for the off outside the Compasses, Littley Green (a teetotaller, Sonny always waited outside). (Author's Photo)

such as the insertion of grills in the rear doors for ventilation, for which a work party was arranged to meet at Bernard Henderson's house, and Peter Blacklock prepared a drivers' rota to assist in getting hounds to meets to help Phemie, a sensible move in view of distances.

In October the Committee accepted Roy Lawrence's suggestion of a day cap of 15p charged to members at each meet to augment funds, but by November this was discontinued and the cap increased to £1 instead. There was even talk of a levy on members of £10 towards the end of the season as there was a currently projected shortfall of £800 by then.

Before Christmas there was a meet at the White Hart, Stebbing and the Fox at Shalford Green, both in the North Essex country: subsequently, further meets in that country in the New Year were carded for the Red Lion, Stambourne; the Fox & Hounds, Thaxted; Bardfield End Green; the Plough, White Notley; the Compasses, Littley Green; and the Plough, Radwinter – the Mid Essex were enjoying the new venues to the full. It was good country and a change from the rather flat land that the Mid Essex were used to in the south of Essex.

In January 1975 it was found that the funds were still almost up to the overdraft limit, though slightly helped by a lump subscription from the North Essex with respect to meets held in their country by the Mid Essex, for which

A meet in the Easters. Author, Denis Counsell, Author's wife and Mary Turner (Author's collection – Stuart Turner photo)

North Essex members were not capped. There was concern that a Hunt Ball at the Heybridge might not show a profit as people had become dis-satisfied with the venue so it was decided to take up Derick Sander's offer of Hutton Hall, this time for a small private dance to be held there. Derick Sanders, a local solicitor and keen supporter of hunting had occasionally come out to follow hounds and generously offered the use of the Hall at Hutton, and much needed funds resulted from a very enjoyable evening in delightful surroundings. He had first been introduced to the Mid Essex Beagles by the author, subsequently one of his partners, who disliked going into the office on a Saturday morning and casually mentioned that the beagles would be meeting at Ingatestone on the Saturday after Christmas and it would be worth going to the meet. The result was the office remained closed that Saturday and Derick Sanders turned out for a much more enjoyable day's exercise, though narrowly missing a ducking in the River Wid after charging through a gap in a hedge which masked the river bank. After that he came out on various Saturdays, sometimes cubbing with foxhounds as well as he liked to keep a horse which he exercised daily.

The Farmers' Supper at Roxwell village hall had two guests, the Principal of Writtle Agricultural College and Maj. the Rev. Phillip Wright both of whom were always good value. Philip Wright had long been a contributor to farming and country magazines. Somewhat eccentric, the Rector of Roxwell turned up to the parish meet of the Essex Hunt mounted upon a skewbald that would have done service at Agincourt, with the local bobbie in attendance on his noddy bike apprehensive for the public safety as the beast cavorted about. In the summer he

Maj. The Rev. Phillip Wright at an Essex Foxhound meet at Newney Green (Author's Photo)

could be seen driving the same horse between the shafts of a trap, through the lanes in the neighbouring parishes. At the Farmers' Supper he told risqué stories in dialect, which brought the house down for he was a great favourite with the farmers.

The overdraft was just about holding its own. However, inoculation fees for $22\frac{1}{2}$ couple of hounds were expected in the summer and would reduce the profit made on the dance and the Grand National Draw. Once more Derick Carlisle was instructed to apply for registration of more country within the Essex Foxhounds country formerly hunted by the North Essex. This would give greater scope for hounds and might attract more members.

During the June AGM Phemie Angus was reporting $21\frac{1}{2}$ brace had been taken in 33 days hunting during the season and she was most grateful to Sonny Davey for his help whipping in on Wednesdays. He had been a whip in the early days of the hunt but still covered the ground better than most and enjoyed his beagling. The subscription was increased to £25. The 1975 accounts shew hound expenses had doubled, kennel rent was up, another hound van had been purchased: at the start of the financial year a surplus of £240 sounded fine, though at its end the accounts stood at £1.76 in hand – even Mr.Macawber would have blenched. The Treasurer forecast that £1,750 was needed by the end of the 1975/6 season to balance the books and reduce the overdraft to £450. Hounds at Barton were well looked after by the Poiles but the increased costs of rent and feed still needed to be covered. A Supper Dance was arranged. The Treasurer suggested a '100 Club' be set up. Unfortunately, it was later found on enquiry that it was not feasible with so small a membership.

The North Essex had at last agreed to the registration by the Mid Essex of the East Essex Foxhound country within the former North Essex boundaries, and offered meets in their remaining country for the 1975/6 season. Though none was to be on the meet cards before Christmas the first meet in the New Year was carded for White House Farm, Stebbing and another meet took place at the Three Horseshoes, Bannister Green, whilst the rest of the season was made up of old Mid Essex favourites.

At the December Committee meeting the overdraft was down to £429, and £600 the assessed figure for running expenses at the end of April 1976. Jack Poile had announced his retirement as Trinity Foot kennel huntsman and there was also a threat of roadworks to the kennel site at Barton, though this might be several years away. The Committee decided to proceed with the written appeal on the Clavering kennels – this had been in abeyance for some time as Phemie had thought her parents might move to another property, where planning would be easier for kennelling. However, it was essential to try an appeal in view of the insecure Barton position. Phemie felt she would like to keep a closer eye on hounds and wanted them at home in Clavering. Although not within the country, with the M11 being constructed it meant that Clavering was not too long a journey to most meets and the Canewdon meet was probably the farthest. However, the planning would have to be dealt with and any objections locally. This meant Phemie would have to appoint an agent, so she set about it.

Again a Hunt Dance was held at Hutton Hall in February, Derick Sanders readily agreeing to let the hunt use the Hall. The estimated expenditure for the 1976/7 season shot up to £2,250 due to an increase in the new kennel huntsman's wages and other expenses. The results of the appeal were still awaited though the feeling was of optimism.

A further blow came with the unexpected death of Frank Fitzwilliam during his fifth term as chairman on the 20th March 1976. He was ever the optimist, and when beagling cheerfully proclaimed he had the best of both worlds for as soon as hunting finished the trout fishing season began; when that ceased he was back to beagling once more. His death created problems for the hunt but Peter Hopton, who had been vice-chairman for some time, was very quickly there to fill the breach and serve as the new chairman. About the same time Richard Hilder was invited to join the committee so that the experience he brought in could be used to advantage.

Peter Hopton called an Emergency Meeting in April 1976 to discuss the new kennels at the Master's house at Clavering becoming a probability rather than a possibility as details for planning and building regulation permissions had emerged and building estimates were awaited. Uttlesford District Council, the authority responsible for planning in the area had already refused the application on the following grounds:

> *The Council consider that dog kennels, either for boarding or breeding, should be located where they do not interfere with the amenities of nearby residential properties. In the Council's opinion, the use of this land as proposed for the accommodation of a hunting pack of beagle hounds would be detrimental to the amenities of the nearby residents by reason of noise and general disturbance caused by the hounds and the traffic which would be generated'.*

Tony Hawkins finally retired from his joint mastership of the Mid Essex having been involved as Master for 24 years, a long run for anyone though nothing like Phemie Angus's 37 years. He handed over hounds to Phemie upon one stipulation that *'should the pack ever be given up only she and I would decide how, and to whom, and in what way they would be disposed of.'* (Tony Hawkins's actual words). Assurances were given to him that the Committee had no claim whatever upon the pack. Phemie was able to say that a tally of 29 brace was reached in 40 days hunting with only one blank day and she had been helped on Wednesdays by Sonny Davey and Derick Carlisle whipping in. Between Jack Poile's retirement and the new kennel huntsman's appearance on the 1st May the Masters of both packs had done the work in kennels – a month of hard work, thankfully after hunting had finished. Just over a fortnight after the AGM the Department of the Environment gave a decision in writing for the proposed kennels. Everyone was overjoyed to hear it had found in Phemie's favour, or rather her father's, for the application had been in his name. Phemie made a written appeal to members for support. Undeterred the Mid Essex duly backed her. The committee thought it would be necessary to raise £2,500 to £3,000 for the project.

Colin Miller in a circular to members gave news of additional country newly registered. Previously North Essex Foot had hunted part of the land north of Little Waltham but with the North Essex joining with the de Burgh Bassetts their country was split. Part they took with them but Derek Carlisle, with the help of Richard Hilder the founder of the North Essex, persuaded them to part with the rest and Derek negotiated with Air Commodore Leslie Levis, the Association's Registrar of Countries, for official recognition of the accession. This gave a good piece of country to hunt now that urban pressure was increasing in the south of the Mid Essex country and ensured continuity for many years to come. Future meets would be held at Bannister Green, Littley Green, Leighs Priory, White Notley, Panfield, Gosfield, Blackmore End, Shalford Green and a whole host of new venues. No longer was it possible to hunt south of Brentwood other than Warren Squires's land at Rochford and around Canewdon. The new country was mainly arable producing very strong hares, and in some cases too many, especially around Panfield. With a new list of meets it also meant new pubs to try

Leez Priory. An excellent meet venue with fantastic entertainment. (Author's photo)

Leez Priory – Michael Mason reports to the Master. (Author's Photo)

Warren Squier & Derick Carlisle at Fristling Hall (Phemie Angus Collection)

and also the teas to arrange for hungry beaglers after covering miles following hounds. The Secretary arranged tea at one of the new meets which was at a pub on the A131. Unknown to the beaglers the emphasis was on the restaurant facilities and not on the bar. Consequently a whole bunch of tired, thirsty, dirty beaglers were welcomed by the proprietor immaculate in black coat and pin striped trousers who then proceeded to ply them with cups of tea and little

Invitation Meet at Waggon & Horses Sheepcote Green Clavering. L to R: Roddy Edwards, Phemie Angus, Peter Green, Roger Dence (Phemie Angus Collection)

sandwiches and minute cakes. Even the W.I. might have felt short changed! Collin Miller remembers the original teas in earlier years cost 2s. 6d. (12½p) in the 1950s, and if alcohol was wanted before 6 p.m. then the curtains were carefully drawn. The profit made from a beagle tea by the proprietor's wife was well worth it in the days before public houses supplied food with drink.

Air Cdre. Leslie Levis had been Registrar of Countries to the Association for many years sitting in judgment over cases rather like a High Court Judge, for his decision was final. Any Masters of harriers or beagles wishing to claim additional country over which they wished to hunt had to put forward to him the facts and arguments: whilst opposers had to do the same. He did not suffer slipshod submissions and expected a case to be argued succinctly. At Hound Conferences he was able to relax and enjoy meeting people from other hunts over dinner or at a local hotel bar in the evening, for when the Per Ardua Beagles were a Royal Air Force pack he was Master and was well able to discuss all matters concerning a pack.

At the October Committee Meeting the Treasurer warned that income would be insufficient for the coming season and by February 1977 a levy would have to be considered, and new meets in the new country were needed to stimulate potential new members. He also advocated a 'shooting members' subscription for February and March after the shooting had finished as beagling was becoming an alternative sport for them for the rest of the season. In November the Agents had estimated the cost of kennels to be in the region of £5,000 if work was done by a contractor and they were asked to produce more detailed drawings for estimates to be obtained. It was decided the first thing to do was to obtain an estimate for the kennel's concrete base and drainage. It has to be remembered that Phemie Angus, Peter Hopton, Roy Lawrence, and many other members had helped in the kennels at Spurriers not just with hounds, but also with maintenance, repair and improvements; the members were not exactly new to kennel problems and knew the pitfalls and what to avoid at all costs.

Mrs. Fitzwilliam was elected an honorary member of the hunt as a tribute to her late husband and in recognition of what she had personally done for the hunt. This met with universal approval for she and her husband had always warmly welcomed the beaglers in their house at Old Harlow, and the members were very fond of them both.

Finances in the meantime had become stretched with an overdraft running for the first time in the hunt's history and an extraordinary general meeting was

```
MID-ESSEX BEAGLES  meet as follows


     1977                    ALL AT 11.30 AM

  Wed    2 March    Woodham Ferrers, The Bell
  Sat    5   "      Chignal Smealey, Pig & Whistle
  Wed    9   "      Moreton, The Nag's Head
  Sat   12   "      Battlesbridge, The Barge
  Wed   16   "      Galleywood, Parklands Farm
  Sat   19   "      Little Baddow, The Rodney
  Wed   23   "      Littley Green, The Compasses
  Sat   26   "      Boreham, The Queen's Head
                    (to close the Season)


  Sat   26 March    The Grand National Draw will take place

  Wed   20 April    Farmers' Supper - details will be sent


              Meet Sec:S.F.Carlisle    Hon.Sec.:C.N.MILLER
  Kennels:    Chelmsford 71033                             Gt Dunmow
```

Meet Card March 1977

called. (Peter Hopton's letter is set out opposite.) The situation was critical, the rent made a hole in funds to a great extent and the subscriptions and additions raised from dances, draws, and other inspirational fund raising was just not going to perform miracles: it was essential for an emergency appeal to be made to members for an extra £30 per head. It was to clear the overdraft and rent. The members responded well.

The 1976/7 season saw Derick Carlisle producing meet cards throughout that period with popular venues which attracted much support, hounds covering Littley Green, Beezly End, Mashbury, Shalford Green, and Moreton over to Galleywood, Little Baddow, Boreham; then further east to West Hanningfield, Woodham Ferrers, Battlesbridge, Woodham Walter, Canewdon, Rochford; and back around Chelmsford to Chignall Smealy, Margaretting Tye, Paslow Common, and Willingale.

In April 1977 a May Day dance was held at Hutton Hall, the venue for the supper dance in the two previous years which had been such a success. By June the AGM considered ways and means of raising funds, some suggestions being a Cheese and Wine Party, a barbecue, a raffle of a bottle of wine at selected meets, reduced audit fee, BFSS Film and quiz, review of Boxing Day cap, 'Race Meeting' evening, hunt supper and Farmers' Supper. Not all of these bore fruit, but it was a start.

The AGM on the 10th June 1977 was probably one of the most momentous in the history of the pack. 1977 also saw Colin Miller resigning as secretary on moving out of the country. He had held the post for 18 years, and it was odd not having him welcoming newcomers at meets and tactfully explaining to them

14 March 1977

MID ESSEX BEAGLES

Message to all Subscribers

THE FUTURE OF THE MID ESSEX IS IN GRAVE DANGER!

Dear Member

As you know, we lost our most able and loyal Chairman, Frank Fitzwilliams, last year, and I mentioned at the AGM that after we had re-formed the Committee and settled down, the whole situation of the Mid Essex Beagles would have to be considered. At that time the situation with the hounds at Barton was known to be unsatisfactory. For this reason we continued to press for planning permission to build kennels at the Master's home and obtained estimates as to the possible financial cost of such a venture. Planning permission has been obtained and from the estimates so far available the cost of the work to meet hound requirements, building regulations and environmental considerations, would be in the region of £3,500. This money would have to be raised by us all and, unless it is to be an impossible financial burden, the money would have to be in the form of interest-free loans over a period of, say, seven years. To this end the Committee are endeavouring to arrange an appropriate agreement for the tenancy of the land and at the same time we are now having to consider whether or not we, as a small group of individuals, are able to finance this major project with confidence and with hope for the future.

The following paragraphs supplied by our Treasurer, Mr Bostridge, give a clear, concise picture of our financial position.

"For some time now the Hunt has worked on overdraft facilities to finance the van purchase. Now our landlords' (the Trinity Foot Beagles) increased rent has provided an additional burden, apart from rising overheads generally. Because of this the Hunt has to find £1,152.00 by the end of April, to start next season from 1st May with a clear bank balance. The aim has been to keep subscriptions down to encourage new membership and to raise money from the Draw and the Dance, and in any other way possible. However, even with this help we are a long way from breaking even, and we now require the sum of £30.00 per subscriber to be raised individually to clear our debt.

"It is estimated that next season at Barton will cost us between £2,250.00 and £2,500.00 per annum. Subscriptions at the current rate would bring in about £1,050.00, so we will still have to find a further £1,450.00, otherwise the Hunt cannot continue."

As will be seen, whether we stay at Barton or whether we are able to fend for ourselves, the financial burden will be considerably increased year by year, due mainly to inflation and the responsibility for repaying any loans which we are able to attract.

To ensure that with a membership of only 34 subscribers we can carry on, the possible subscription, without new fund-raising events, could be in the region of £70 per year, and therefore we particularly need new members.

I do not think it too strong to say that the position is critical, and unless the Committee and our Master have the tangible support of all subscribers, it is very obvious that we are going to fall more deeply into debt. The Committee are at present considering what can be done to activate new membership, attract more money, expand meets and, if possible, increase the number of subscribers by a discreet campaign of recruitment.

I would ask all of you to pay a levy of £30 per subscriber, or an amount to suit your pocket, to be sent as soon as possible to the Treasurer, in order to meet our immediate debts.

In conclusion, I would impress upon everybody that this is a matter of grave concern to all those interested in the continuation of the Mid Essex and the fine sport which has been shown by Miss Angus for many years, and which has involved her in a considerable personal and financial sacrifice. I would welcome any support and suggestions that you can make. Please let me have these on the attached form (via the Treasurer). A stamped, addressed envelope is enclosed.

To discuss all these points urgently, an extraordinary general meeting will be held on MONDAY, 28 MARCH, at 8 pm at THE GRANGE, FRYERNING (by kind permission of Mr and Mrs B Clark). Please attend if at all possible.

Yours sincerely

Peter Hopton

Chairman

Sonny Davey with Phemie and Roddy Edwards at Moreton (Stuart Turner Collection)

Phemie and hounds at Moreton, '77 (Stuart Turner Collection)

West Hanningfield – The Compasses. This meet was for the East Hanningfield Reservoir area – not the place to be in thick fog! (Clive Petchey Collection)

Colin Miller with Michael Mason at West Hanningfield. (Author's Photo)

The Pig & Whistle, Chignall Smealy. One of the best in the early years until sold to newcomers. (Author's Photo)

Barry Clark with Tony Kidd. (Author's Photo)

Peter Spital with Phemie and hounds. (Phemie Angus Collection)

what was to happen if they had not beagled before. His place was taken by the writer and Christopher Latham was elected Treasurer. Derek Carlisle resigned after having been meet secretary for 8 years and he and his wife, Joan, another keen beagler moved up to Suffolk. The writer subsequently took on Derek's work as well. During the season the tally had been $21^1/2$ brace in 33 days' hunting and $3^1/2$ couple of puppies had been bred and still a shortage of volunteer puppy walkers. To everyone's regret news was received that after his retirement both Jack Poile and his wife had died. They had been good friends to Phemie and the Mid Essex and many of the members had fond memories of their welcome to tea at Barton. The Chairman bluntly drew a picture of failing finances, the Trinity Foot wanted more rent, the members had not raised sufficient despite the appeal to clear the deficit by a levy, and with a subscription list of only 30 members there was a limit to what could be raised from outside functions. The kennel project could go no further without additional funds. Phemie had told members she hoped the pack could continue and certainly she would give two years' notice of any intention to run it down and would definitely continue for the coming season; she reckoned Barton would be available for the next two years, though road building could cause its closure. Brent Pelham, the Puckeridge Foxhound kennels, would have the Mid Essex but that would involve the kennelman looking after foxhounds and beagles. In fact, a gloomy picture, indeed.

In September Christopher Latham, exercising his authority as treasurer, wrote the members setting out the subscription details and for the first time shooting members could pay a reduced subscription for February and March, after shooting had finished. A new venue was sought for the hunt ball in order to increase profits by holding a larger function with reliance on selling tickets to outsiders and Furze Hill, Margaretting was chosen.

To help Phemie, Michael Mason was appointed Field Master in 1978 to better control the field out hunting. Michael had been joint master of the Sproughton Foot from 1970–74 so he knew what was involved. News of the financial crisis reached the local press who blazoned in large letters '**HUNT FACING CASH CRISIS**' across the article written up for the occasion. In another local paper there was a naive article full of misquotations after various officers of the hunt had been interviewed which made everyone cringe. It became clear that one had to be extremely guarded in what one said during interviews, and yet the press could be a great ally if treated fairly and the publicity could be beneficial to the hunt. Certainly this became important in later years.

From the commencement of hunting the pack meets had been traditionally at 11.30 am but now changed to 12 o'clock sharp: those who liked a half pint before setting off could still turn up at 11.30, as long as they realised 12 o'clock start meant just that. The season opened with the usual pre-Christmas meets, with the opening meet at the Bell, Willingale and on the Saturday just before Christmas week an unusual meet in Haslingfield, Cambridgeshire by invitation within the Trinity Foot country. Boxing Day saw a large field and many well wishers appearing at the Bull, Blackmore. By February the King William IV at

Navestock saw hounds gathering and in March a meet was carded by invitation at the Wagon & Horses, Clavering in the Puckeridge country. To end the season hounds met at the Queen's Head, Boreham.

The Farmers' Supper was held at Roxwell Village Hall where the members wives helped to lay the tables and behind the scenes make it a very good evening. With a raffle the Supper made a profit, though without the wives' help it is doubtful if it would have been such a success. The Secretary's report afterwards mentioned that Major the Reverend Philip Wright was unwell and unable to attend. It was a blow not to have the hunting vicar of Roxwell as an after dinner speaker. For the first time Phemie attended as Master, though not the only lady for one who farmed exercised her right as well. In fact 30 farmers, 6 official guests, and 36 members and friends attended. Colin Miller was presented with an engraved decanter and, in absentia, Derek Carlisle with a mounted model hare.

The Treasurer was relieved to find the previous year's deficit was extinguished and the year would end with a small surplus of £40. This was no mean achievement on his part, the result of hard work, and chivvying voluntary helpers in the raising of funds, giving them encouragement where needed, and not letting his exasperation show where some hoped for events had not taken place or produced as much profit as anticipated. Christopher Latham had already put up the subscription to £36 and now wanted to keep it to that figure for the coming season but the Committee decided to endorse his management of the funds by increasing it to £40, no family subscription, £2 meet card charge for non-members and the cap now to be £1.50.

The AGM in June was held at the home of Tony and Pam Kidd. There it was decided to make available gilt hunt club lapel buttons and sets of waistcoat buttons. These became very popular and provided some profit. The end of season balance was £98. Unfortunately the members had to be castigated later for not sufficiently supporting the Race Night or the 'Trad Jazz' and Fish 'n Chips evening arranged by two members: the former was cancelled and the latter only just made a profit with the help of outsiders, (Tony Kidd volunteered to collect the fish and chips, aided by Bernard Henderson, forgetting the powerful aroma of fish and chips for 30 people or so might have a lingering effect on the interior

Hunt Club button

of his car, – no one asked him for a lift to the next few meets!). At the AGM the annual subscription was confirmed at £40 with the cap fixed at £1.50. whilst the meet card would now cost £3. The Mid Essex had long been the second most expensive pack of beagles in the country and there was no indication this dubious reputation was going to change. The list of subscribers had always been somewhat short and it was a chicken and egg situation: lower subscriptions might encourage more members but it might not bring in the numbers hoped for, leaving the funds even more stretched. A treasurer's nightmare. The hunt ball had made a good profit under Christopher and Jacqueline Latham's direction with Roderick Edwards running the raffle, and the Farmers' Supper was well supported with the attendance of 6 official guests, 27 farmers (150 invited), and 36 members and friends. Rent at the Trinity Foot kennels was up again. The Master, despite the van breaking down, managed 36 days hunting and a total of 20 brace of hares.

In the months leading up to the start of the 1978/9 season several committee meetings deliberated upon the kennel details. It seemed that for breeze block and rendered buildings the cost would be in the region of £3,000 to £5,000: If Elm loose boxes were used it could be reduced to £2,500. Unitary constructed buildings had been found by other hunts to be too damp. An estimate of £600 a year was put forward for actually keeping hounds, to include flake maize and calor gas. If second hand loose boxes could be found the initial cost of erecting kennels might be reduced to about £1,700 to £2,000. There were reserve matters in the planning approval which had yet to be cleared with the local planning officer and it looked like the end of April before work could be started. Phemie Angus told the Committee if a decision to kennel at Clavering had not been reached by the end of the season she would be forced to run down the pack over the following two seasons. Subsequently in March 1979 the Committee received further figures: £800 for loose boxes, £3,420 or £2,248 for concreting, drainage and septic tank only, excluding erection of buildings, yard walls and electricity and water supplies. The Treasurer now had to revise his financial calculations from £2,900 to £4,000 total cost. An Extraordinary General Meeting was called on the 29th April 1979 at the home of Christopher and Jacqueline Latham. Peter Hopton, as Chairman, outlined the financial requirements for the new kennels and stressed that the Trinity Foot had asked for more rent and a grant towards capital expenditure. He pointed out that if the new kennels were to be erected with the help of a bank loan this would be at 16% p.a., the current rate on this type of loan and hinted that there could be savings in having their own kennels. The Master guaranteed to keep hunting for at least five years if at Clavering; otherwise could only keep them for a further two years, and added that a new van would be needed, too. The Treasurer then launched an appeal for loans and gifts saying he wanted to see £3,000 in the bank straightaway. By the end of the meeting he had offers of £900 inloans and gifts of £1,270, not what he had hoped for, but a start. A fortnight later the total promised was £2,600, not enough as yet to relax, though in June Christopher having promises of £3,085 felt it was possible to go ahead, especially as detailed planning consent was now through, for he knew that if a further £115 was received he had been assured the balance needed would be made up in increased promises.

That season there had been some problems with anti-hunt saboteurs in the old North Essex country and police assistance had been required. The BFSS had started a campaign to prevent hunting being banned by statute and members were asked to canvas election candidates. This was an ongoing activity for the next 27 years. Phemie Angus was invited to judge hounds at the Honiton Show which she thoroughly enjoyed. It was quite an honour which the members appreciated.

The 1978/9 season cards, (apart from the early morning meets, one of which was at Fristling Hall, Stock), all shewed noon as the starting time. For a change the opening meet was at the Black Horse, Paslow Common, Boxing Day being at the Bull, Blackmore. On the 3rd February the Bell at Panfield had been selected, a meet later becoming renowned for a surfeit of hares. To close the season the Fox at Mashbury had been selected and once more a memorable tea was available.

Again the members held their AGM at Tony and Pam Kidd's house in June 1979. Peter Hopton had decided to give up the chairmanship and passed it over to Barry Clark. Peter had held office during difficult times and guided the hunt well. Christopher Latham was keeping a tight hand on finances and forecast a saving of £650 per annum if kennels could be built at Clavering. In actual fact most of this would be down to Phemie Angus acting as her own kennelman, not taking holidays and no doubt subsidising her own hounds in other ways. It would require a great deal of dedication. Peter Hopton had suggested a sub-committee be appointed for the kennel building project. The Master reported that hounds had hunted well for 24 days with a tally of 12 brace. She asked for puppy walkers as she hoped to have some puppies later in the year. She also suggested that meets should not be advertised after foxhunting had finished as it attracted the attention of hunt saboteurs who became a nuisance about 1977. Roger Flint became assistant secretary as the writer found organising meets was very time consuming, especially when great tact was needed with a certain ancient Master of Foxhounds who placed every difficulty in the way and in time this was only overcome by requesting a meet which was not wanted, on the predictable answer being 'No', and the aged Master offering an alternative which was invariably what was wanted in the first place. Most Masters were very co-operative indeed. Shooters were unpredictable and badly organised in some cases, though farmers arranging their own shoots were very helpful.

Liz Porter's kaleidoscopic memories include endeavouring to collect up hounds in the dusk which moved away just as one got to them; Phemie checking in hounds at the end of the day with the help of a piece of card torn from a cornflake packet (dog hounds scribbled on one side, bitches on the other) – they all seemed to look up when their names were called; her son Dominic when whipping in tapping on a frozen pond with the handle of his whip until the tip of the bone broke: burying at home, by torch light, a hound killed by running

Phemie with hounds at Fristling Hall (Stuart Turner Collection)

Fristling Hall meet (Stuart Turner Collection)

into a car; sheltering under a tree at Galleywood on a freezing snowy day; Phemie's keenness to teach any youngster who shewed an interest in hunting; Sonny Davie, ever immaculate and driving a spotless car to the meet whatever the weather, and Roddy Edwards occasionally whipping in by car with a cigarette alight and a pint of beer on the passenger seat, emerging to crack a whip and turn an errant hound at the appropriate moment.

Now the Clavering kennelling was at last under way. A Building sub-committee was formed consisting of Phemie Angus, Peter Spital as Secretary/Treasurer, Roderick Duncan to supervise building and Michael Mason. Peter Spital was to instruct the builder to proceed and to order the loose boxes which would be erected by volunteers, whilst Christopher Latham arranged for transportation of the loose boxes from works to site. The aim was to complete the project by the last day of October. For the time being the Committee put the kennel fund on building society deposit.

Before September the last of the reserved matters and building regulation approvals had been dealt with or obtained. It would be tight but possible. The concrete base was down, a spare kennel and boundary wire had been delivered and a date fixed for the delivery of the looseboxes by Christopher, and Peter Spital was to arrange for off-loading. Building blocks were on their way. Roderick Duncan had run a disco in aid of the fund and made £108 which was a bonus, this could help towards the provision of feed bins and tools. By the beginning of October the loose boxes had been erected by Roderick Duncan, and Barry Clark had the metal lining sheets lined up. The block walls had been built by contract labour and part of the fence for the grass run. Some additional cost had been

*Again at Fristling Hall
(Stuart Turner Collection)*

incurred with labour and plant hire resulting in the final overall cost amounting to £3,960. Phemie had arranged the kennel insurance and all that remained to be done was the rest of the fencing and pipe laying. The re-roofing of the ancillary sheds had yet to be completed and then hounds could move in.

Roderick Duncan (whip), Denis Counsell in background. (Author's Photo)

Stuart Turner taking a break (Author's Collection)

CHAPTER 5

One More Check
– The Last Move

Hounds were moved to their new quarters and the small balance of rent paid to the Trinity Foot for an additional 41 days kennelling. The kennel huntsman of the Trinity Foot was given a Christmas present. The sharing of kennels with the Trinity Foot had proved an enormous help after the Otterhounds could no longer stay at Little Totham, but it was a relief to have hounds permanently in their own home and under the eye of the Master. In December, Phemie gave an interesting estimate of costs:

60 bibles (paunches which were boiled up)	£13.20 per week
Dried meat	£2 per week
Maize	£2.50 per week
Straw	£1 per week
Shavings	£1.50 per week
Total	£21 per week

On top of this there were General and Water Rates, veterinary fees (a lucky dip at the best of times) and, as time went on, ongoing repairs and improvements (it was found that an overflow storm drain was needed). Also a concrete path was wanted from the house down to the kennels, and guttering.

The Committee pursued fund raising with vigour. Peter Blacklock was in charge of the Grand National Draw; Christopher Latham was running a Boxing Day meet Champagne raffle; the ladies' sub-committee formed by Brenda Clark were preparing details of the Farmers' Supper for which Peter Hopton generously supplied the meat and stilton and John Grundy produced the cutlery and linen; Peter Hopton was arranging the printing of the Hunt Ball tickets, whilst Christopher Latham was settling the choice of menu at the Meads Ballroom.

Meets were no longer being advertised in the local press or shop windows in order to keep details out of the antis' hands and the Chief Constable was receiving a meet card so that the local police knew the hunt's movements for intelligence purposes. Cancellation of meets and change of venues caused a problem resulting in a list of members being converted into an emergency phoning pyramid, so that if the Master cancelled or changed by 9 a.m. the phoning around went into operation thereafter and in theory all members would be aware within minutes. Often it was the case that the meet had to be cancelled due to extremes of winter weather, or sometimes, the night before, a panic call from a foxhound master might be received by the meet secretary to ask if a change of venue could be made as the foxhounds needed the meet because their own had been cancelled. One had to keep the Foxhound Masters happy for, after all, it was their country we hunted over by courtesy.

The Pig & Whistle was a welcome meet to open the season in November 1979 with the Bull, Blackmore once again being chosen for the Boxing Day meet. The early months of 1980 consisted of the most popular meets, though a new one was the King's Head, Gosfield, and for the closing meet the Compasses, West Hanningfield was chosen.

The new Kennels at Phemie Angus's home. (Author's Photo)

Two followers in conversation. Tony Lewis and Michael Beale. (Author's Photo)

Some of the Field. L. to R. – Tony Kidd, Brig. Jerry Finch, Barbara Bostridge, Brenda Clark, Stuart and Mary Turner, other two unknown. (Author's Photo)

By June 1980 when the AGM was held at Christopher and Jacqueline Lathams' house The meeting was packed and the atmosphere was bullish for Barry Clark announced that 70% of the cost of the new kennels had been raised through gifts and the remainder by long term loans. The Master reckoned that hounds had taken some time to settle in after the move and there had been some problems in the early part of the season with the splitting of the pack due to exceedingly good scenting conditions, though this had not stopped them from hunting on 32 days and accounting for 18 brace of hare. There was talk of the Master giving lectures to the field, many of whom were new to beagling, so they knew what to do if the pack split. It was decided to give them a booklet on beagling instead, and in any event Roy Lawrence was responsible for educating the whips under instruction so it was better to leave it to the whips to sort out.

The Hunt Ball under Christopher Latham's guidance notched up £300 profit and the Farmers' Supper a profit of £95 mainly due to a generous gift of food by Peter Hopton and the loan of plates and cutlery by John Grundy with resulting cost saving. It was noted that 200 invitations had been sent out and 30

Meet at Jericho Priory, the home of the late Ted Marriage, father of the late Betty Gingell of Cambridgeshire Harriers fame. Ted Marriage used to hold Sunday polo matches on a meadow opposite the Priory. (Author's Photo)

Barry and Brenda Clark, both of whom gave a great deal of help for many years to the pack as Chairman and organiser of social events respectively. (Brenda Clark Collection)

Hunting along the banks of Hanningfield Reservoir. (Author's Collection)

A weak scenting day at the Reservoir. (Author's collection)

farmers attended. Perhaps it sounds as if farmers were not interested in coming but the gesture had been made and that they appreciated. To produce more money for the following season Peter Blacklock volunteered to run a 100 Club. He had already run a Grand National Draw the previous season. Inflation was biting hard and so subscriptions were raised to £45 an individual, £65 for family and the cap increased to £2.

Roger Flint and the writer became joint secretaries. This was only right and proper for Roger was carrying out most normal secretary's business leaving meets the sole preserve of Peter Bostridge. Roy Lawrence had clocked up 25 years as a whip and to mark it Phemie presented him with a picture to shew her personal appreciation for all his work.

The poor old hound van was in a bad way but it was decided to put off the day when it would have to be consigned to the scrap yard, at least for another season, by carrying out repairs to the bodywork. Modern vehicles without chassis were much more subject to rust where hounds were concerned, the steam emitting from close packed bodies and hounds relieving themselves in the straw on the floor of the van took its toll over the years. With the regulations requiring MOT tests annually were coupled those needing the vehicle to be steam cleaned each time prior to the test. The staff of the garage where this was done always reckoned it was one of their least enjoyable duties.

Peter Blacklock's 100 Up Club, by November, shewed a £230 profit, 68 members having subscribed to 75 shares in the venture, and the Wine and Cheese party had made a £75 profit.

In January 1981 the hunt ball was held at Furze Hill, Margaretting which gave more room and reasonable surroundings. During the summer just before

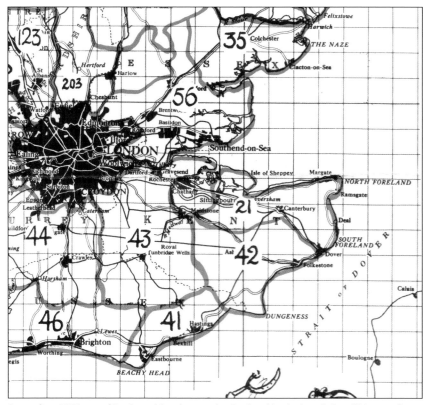

Extract from 1980 map of Harrier and Beagle countries. Produced by the Association of Masters of Harriers and Beagles (by kind permission of the Association). Mid Essex country no. 56.

the AGM the chairman sent out his annual report. Once again the financial situation was critical due to increased veterinary costs, feed and van maintenance. The committee had asked the Master to reduce the number of hounds, this she refused to do on the grounds that she did not wish to dispose of good hounds and felt she could not hunt so successfully with a smaller pack. The alternative was to increase the subscription to £50 and cap hound related expenditure so that the Master would be responsible for any additional costs. Again the Master dug in her heels; she argued that even though the expenditure might well be within the capped sum she might have to make up the moneys out of her own pocket if it were not so (It must be remembered that she had already found some of the previous season's hound costs herself, she was her own kennelman saving the hunt moneys and was with hounds practically 24 hours a day). This created an impasse to be sorted out at the AGM.

On the plus side there had been an increase in members, the hunt ball was a success due to Christopher and Jacqueline Lathams' organisation backed up by Michael and Cynthia Masons' Tombola, so that Furze Hill was booked again for the next year with the same band. The 100 club was a distinct success and a wine and cheese party and several raffles were productive too. The farmers' Supper at Roxwell Village Hall was a good draw despite clashing with Easter.

A sum of money had been collected to purchase a pair of spurs as a leaving present for Roderick Duncan, but he had already gone to take up an apprenticeship with Capt. Ronnie Wallace's Exmoor Foxhounds near Simonsbath close to the Somerset border with Devon. The writer happened to be going down to Exford for fishing and to follow staghounds in May, so on a very snowy day he duly handed over the spurs to Roderick who, with various other youths, was housed in chilly quarters heated by a single bar electric fire with an old settee and linoleum covered floors. Tough conditions, especially in that weather but one of the finest schools in the hunting field. It was not surprising that the offer to draw hounds was regretfully turned down; an honour at any other time, but not in thick snow.

At the AGM in June at the Lathams' the Master was reporting that the puppies had entered well and the general health of hounds was very good, although to attain this the veterinary bills had been large. They had hunted on 36 days and accounted for 24 brace which brought the tally up to 595½ brace for the past 26 seasons, an average of 22½ a season overall. In the last season hounds had 3 blank days and 5 hunting days were lost. She mentioned that there were difficulties in arranging some meets owing to the increased popularity of shooting and the spread of suburbia.

When the Treasurer came to his report he said there were insufficient funds for the start of the next season. This led to the discussion arising out of the Chairman's Report delivered before the AGM. Barry Clark pointed out to members that hounds were the property and sole responsibility of the Master, though it had always been the Committee's responsibility to provide financial support for hounds. He went on to say that the Committee felt it was inappropriate to raise subscriptions by more than £5 to £50 for a single member, and asked the Master to accept a limit on the amount of cash available for hound related expenses. He stated it was a clear choice: either hound numbers should be reduced, or subscriptions increased beyond the Committee's recommendation – already the subscription was the second highest in the country. The Master pointed out that 23½ couple were being supported by Members although she was keeping other hounds at her own expense and could not reduce numbers and hunt the country as she did. The treasurer costed each hound at £50 per annum and he argued a reduction in numbers would show a pro rata reduction in costs. The Master giving a resumé of the feeding programme pointed out one important factor, namely, that because of the proximity of foxhound kennels fallen animals were not available. (The foxhounds would have priority in their country and the Mid Essex were outside the Puckeridge country anyway, and the Association rules preclude accepting flesh in such circumstances unless by agreement with the foxhound masters.) This did greatly affect feeding costs as without this source of food hounds would need alternatives which in turn would put up the cost.

For an hour and a half the arguments flowed backwards and forwards. In the end the members voted to increase the single subscription to £55 , family pro

Evening Count.
(Clive Petchey Collection)

rata, and the resolution to increase the cap to £2.50 did not seem acceptable so it stayed at £2. Everyone was determined to raise moneys with more events and activities.

There had always been shoots within the country organised by the larger landowners and these curtailed hunting in some parts until after 1st. February and were taken into consideration, but smaller farmers realised they had a saleable commodity and decided to cash in on it. They allowed shooters in for an annual payment which from the farmers' points of view provided extra cash, though by so doing created a headache for the hunts as the shooters were not subject to the discipline of the larger shoots and omitted to warn the hunts when a shoot was taking place. It was very frustrating to turn up to a meet to find a shoot already in progress. It was even more so when, unannounced, a voice yelled plaintively from a nearby belt of trees, 'Charley, I've run out of shells. Chuck us a few over.' Thank God Charley was without – a few peppered hounds might have been the result. Taking co-operation to the extreme, some farmers who shot together over each others' farms would telephone on receiving notification of an intended meet to say, 'Come by all means. We'll start early from … and you follow round, we shan't get in each others way – you don't start 'til 1130.' It sounded as if hounds would be half a day behind!

That year the hunt lost a great friend. David Baddeley died to everyone's regret. A keen beagler in his time and chairman in the Hunt's opening years he had made his mark on the Mid Essex and would not be forgotten.

Early morning meets were carded from mid-October and the opening meet took place at the Fox, Mashbury. For a change on Boxing Day hounds met at the Ship, Stock, which was very popular with the holiday crowds and with the publican. The Fox at Mashbury must have been in great favour, for the closing meet was there as well. It certainly was one of the greatest favourites at the time for the teas it put on at the end of the day. The meets in the Easters were always well attended and the farmers in the area included Henry Marriage who hunted with the Essex Foxhounds and also set up the point-to-point course at High Easter with his son Simon, and Tom Pitt always made the beagles welcome as did the Matthews family as well.

Henry Marriage at a meet of the Essex Foxhounds (Author's photo)

CHAPTER 6

The Long Run – The Finest Years

The following year it was clear that the increased subscriptions and an actual reduction in cost of hound upkeep had improved the financial position, several successful supper evenings had been organised by Hazel Davies and Bernard Henderson, the Farmers' Supper had gone well and the Hunt Ball, although attendance was down, had been a success as well. As far as hunting was concerned the 1982/3 season was not good. It had been a hard winter and many meets had to be cancelled. In fact, the Master reported only 14 brace had been accounted for in 18 days hunting and 17 days had been lost. (The meet cards for the season show 39 meets, so actually 21 days had been lost.) The closing meet was at Leez Priory by invitation and it was a handsome venue where followers were entertained magnificently, both before hounds moved off and at tea afterwards. Some of the country was lost through urbanisation and faster roads made it dangerous for hounds, but the Master said she would maintain her promise to give two years notice of when she intended to cease hunting. A sub-committee had been formed by the writer with Mark Melvin (later a Joint Master of the Newmarket Beagles) and Nick Boustead to establish new meets. Phemie was getting assistance around the kennels from a nucleus of members: John Hosford,

Hounds in kennels. (Author's photo)

Friendly's pups 1987 (Phemie Angus Collection)

Peter Spital taking a breather at Beyton Hall. (Hester Davies Collection)

Phemie with hounds as they used to be, and much later with the lighter coloured pack (Author's photo)

Derek Thostle and Owen Taylor helped with hound exercise in the summer and Peter Spital and Mark Melvin did work in kennels themselves.

The accounts were now showing an increased income from subscriptions though a drop in caps, partly owing to loss of meets around Christmas and the New Year due to the weather. In fact there were now 45 members and it looked as if there was a healthy interest. Nevertheless the Treasurer predicted that although veterinary fees would be kept down van expenses would be the menace. He asked for, and got, an increase in subscriptions to £60 a member and £90 family, whilst keeping the card subscription at £5 and the cap at £2. The Hunt Ball was fixed for January 1983, once more at Furze Hill. At the AGM there was some disappointment indicated at cancellation of Wednesday meets due to weather and lack of whips so members were asked to check with kennels beforehand, whilst others complained that new country was needed, and it had to be pointed out to them that it took a lot of work to register new country first, then it had to be opened up with new meets and finally the hunt had to hunt it properly, otherwise run the risk of loosing it to others. Unfortunately whilst many members enjoyed the hunting and the social life they knew little about the general running of a hunt and had to be gently led in the right direction, it was surprising how many were not members of the British Field Sports Society, even chairmen in some cases. By the time of the ban a lot of hunts would not allow anyone to join without proof of their Countryside Alliance membership number.

Phemie Angus had taken 2 couple of hounds to the Essex Agricultural Show and that had been much appreciated. It did no harm to exhibit them to the public and attracted a lot of attention from the children apart from the converted. Shows were becoming more and more an open window for hunting and field sports in general. One of the ongoing problems for the Master was the training of young whips and a shortage of those more experienced. The young were very enthusiastic but needed guidance if they were to be of use in the hunting field later. However, learn they did and some of them became very fine whips indeed.

As had now become his custom Barry Clark sent out his Chairman's Letter in February 1983 but this time calling an Extraordinary Meeting a fortnight later at the Latham's. Finance reared its head once more, and there had been a loss of country, partly due to fast traffic, a shortage of whips and little help in kennels. The meeting would be called to discuss yet another increase in subscriptions and/or levies; or give up hunting. 28 members attended.

Since the season had started it had become apparent that no longer could the country be hunted from the Thames to the sea and up to Sible Hedingham. Gradually over the last 31 years it had been eroded bit by bit until a line east and west of Chelmsford for all practical purpose was the southernmost limit of the huntable country, and even that was no longer feasible in some parts. As the Master confirmed, shortage of experienced whips, fast roads and more shooting were taking their toll. She had herself contributed £360 in the last season towards the running costs of the van and felt it should have a further estimated sum of

£300 spent on it to renew the bodywork, and she was feeding hounds as cheaply as possible.

The Master went on to say that 1982/83 had been a real problem because of weather and control of hounds, though the latter was much improved with help from John Hosford and Mark Melvin but the current season had started late due to trouble with the van and three meets had been missed as a result. She promised to keep hounds at kennels for at least five years and confirmed hunting would continue for a further two years , in effect giving two years notice of termination of hunting should it, in her opinion, no longer be feasible to continue.

Meet in yard at Nether Hall, Moreton. (Author's photo)

Henry Marriage following the Mid Essex over his own land (Author's photo)

Roy Lawrence and Jim Hocking, Roy in 'undress' uniform. (Phemie Angus Collection)

The members argued backwards and forwards and at one point paused to draw breath and have something to eat and drink and talk among themselves. That was a wise move, for a motion ensued to put up the subscription to £75 per member and a levy of £25 if it should be necessary. It was carried, for no one wanted to see the hunt fold up. This must have been one of the longest meetings in the history of the hunt – the minutes recorded that the meeting closed at 10.45 p.m., nearly three hours of strenuous discussion!

When the AGM came round again at the Lathams' in June, it was a much shorter evening and really a reiteration of the problems aired at the previous meeting with one new recommendation from the chairman, namely that a family subscription would include children up to the age of 18 and a reduced student subscription of £25 up to 25 years. The Master, in her resumé, regretted the disappointing season of 32 days with 6 blank, and only 11 brace accounted for and said there was a need for better country and more meets. She was particularly grateful for the support of Dr. Ian and Julia Porter and 'Sonny' Davey whipping in on Wednesday meets. Julia, of course, before her marriage to Ian, had whipped in and 'Sonny' at the time was not only probably the oldest beagler but also the longest serving as he had whipped in for Captain Hawkins in the 1950s.

For some reason there had been no Farmers' Supper. This was a mistake. As a PR exercise it was of paramount importance to run this for annual recognition of the part played by the farmers in the hunting year. It was expected. It had been shewn that it could be run at a profit. Nevertheless the committee, misguidedly in their wisdom, had decided they could not afford it. Instead they concentrated on other events for raising funds, purely and simply. The Hunt Ball had been a great success and the 100 Club was to continue. The increase in subscriptions as agreed at the Emergency Meeting was confirmed.

Roderick Edwards, then a law student, was elected to the committee and the writer relinquished the post of Meet Secretary.

After some time spent by the committee looking for a meet secretary for the following season Michael Mason said he would be prepared to take it on if he could have the assistance of Mark Melvin. Michael had his previous experience as a joint master of the Sproughton Foot in Suffolk to fall back on, Mark had started as a sixteen year old with the pack and had been whipping in for some

Geoff Dignum and Richard Paine deep in discussion. (Hester Davies Collection)

Ken Bartlett and John Bucknall at Fairstead, near Terling. 7th March 1992 (Hester Davies Collection)

Phillip Schneidau and Roy Rodwell (Hester Davies Collection)

time, so that with all this experience with the Mid Essex it was of much value when he later became joint master of the Newmarket Beagles.

Towards the end of September the Committee had decided not to purchase a new body for the van, but to replace it and keep the old one for spare parts. The kennels needed some work, creosoting, clearing of drains and the buying of padlocks for security, whilst a plea for a wheelbarrow and extra brooms was noted: there was no doubt the final move had been a great success. By October a hound van replacement was critical. Without it the hunting season could not get under way. Michael Mason and Mark Melvin had fixed meets up to Christmas but without a van their work would be in vain. Apart from that all fund raising activities, the hunt supper, the 100 Club, and others had to be deferred. The offer of the loan of a horse box had been turned down and there was a suggestion that a van might be hired, but it was gently pointed out to the member suggesting it that there would be a general reluctance on the part of van hire contractors for obvious reasons to let their vehicles out for the transport of hounds! However, at the 11th hour, as happens so often in beagling management a van was purchased allowing the season to start on time, and immediately plans were finalised for a hunt ball, a wine and cheese party and a Christmas dinner to supplement funds. Once more an up-to-date telephone list was prepared to warn of any cancellations of meets. This had proved to be an essential to prevent unnecessary wastage of petrol in attending cancelled meets and ensuing frustration.

Back to the Bell, Willingale for the opening meet on the 29th October 1983, opposite the two churches, and unfortunately there was no meet on Wednesday, the 2nd November and meets had to be changed on the 12th and 19th as well.

Hounds and Field at Tibbles Farm, Hawkedon in Suffolk. 2nd March 1991 (Hester Davies Collection)

Bartlett, Phemie and and Letitia Mason at Fairstead. 7th March 1992 (Hester Davies Collection)

However, by December matters had settled down reasonably well, although confirmation of most January meets was required subsequent to the issue of the meet card. Boxing Day was fixed for the Chequers, Roxwell and once again Leez Priory was favoured for the closing meet.

From January 1984 funds looked at a much better level, though the major problem the hunt now faced was its future, for the Committee were now looking at a further two seasons of hunting before urbanisation caught up making hunting too difficult in much of the country. There had been an attempt to revive the farmers' supper, unfortunately the date fixed clashed with the one given by the Essex Hunt so it had to be aborted. The 100 Club, by the AGM in June, was thought to have run its course and was no longer to be carried on. Peter Hopton

Phemie with Brenda Clark moving off to draw at Shalford in 1993. (Hester Davies Collection)

after many years on the committee and as former chairman had decided to give up the committee and Mark Melvin had to resign as assistant to the Meet Secretary, no longer being able to find the time. For once there was no increase in subscriptions required, for the Treasurer was satisfied with the level of funds, confirming subscriptions at members: £75, Retired Members: £35, Family: £100, Under 25 years: £25. It is worth noting the elected officers for the 1984/5 season were:

Chairman	Barrie Clark
Vice Chairman and Treasurer	Christopher Latham
Joint Secretary (Meets)	Michael Mason
Joint Secretary (Admin.)	Roger Flint
Committee	Peter Spital
	Mark Melvin
	Richard Randall
Auditors	Tony Kidd
	Richard Pain

The last two had carried out the annual audit very efficiently for a number of years.

In the end the Farmers' Supper was fixed for November by Richard Randall and was a resounding success, so too was the Wine and Cheese held by Barrie and Brenda Clark at their home, but Christopher Latham who had organised the Hunt Ball was worried that numbers were down and felt it would have been even lower had not Matthew Pain collected together a large party of guests on the night.

Early morning meets began with the Harringtons' Butt Hatch Farm, Roxwell at 7.30 am. Pat Harrington was a joint master of the Essex Foxhounds so the family always welcomed the beagles on their various farms. The meet cards shewed all the old favourites with the addition of the Axe & Compass, Aythorpe Roding, Fuller Street and a visit by invitation to Clavering for the 1st January, whilst the closing meet was at the Three Horseshoes, Bannister Green, but as Phemie was to say at the AGM quite a few meets were lost.

On the 19th July 1985 at the AGM Phemie Angus reported that traffic was interrupting hunting in the country to such an extent that it was rare for hounds not to be stopped at some stage. The chairman endorsed this saying that below the A12 it was at its worst. Hounds had hunted 16 days and accounted for 8 brace. She went on to say that since the Mid Essex started 35 meet venues had been lost to urbanisation. Phemie had undertaken to give two years' notice if she intended to fold up the pack and the Committee were satisfied to accept this under the circumstances. She was going to investigate with Matthew Pain the possibility of new country. Sonny Davey was still actively beagling despite being over 80 years of age.

Tributes were paid to Warren Squier who had died during the season. He was a noted cricketer and foxhunter who had always been a friend to the Mid Essex and many a meet had taken place at Doggetts, where the hunt was marvellously entertained by the whole family, Warren fiercely backing the hunt to the hilt through all its vicissitudes and generously giving help when needed, with the connection continuing through his son Dan and daughter-in-law Marion right up to the very end of hunting.

Subscriptions were put up by £5 a year to offset increasing costs.

The season started off with the usual meets and a trip to The Wagon & Horses at Clavering for an invitation meet on New Year's Day, but from then on some meets further afield appeared: the Queens Head, Hawkedon for Stansfield on the 18th January and the Crown Hartest on the 1st February. The Pig & Whistle, Chignall Smealy ended the season – twice around the quarry and a good tea afterwards. The Stacey, Towns and Wastney farms each provided their own particular form of country and hares were strong.

In January 1986 talk was of giving up some Mid Essex country and gaining new meets in Suffolk. By March this had been further clarified by the suggestion that three meets a season should be arranged in Suffolk. The Treasurer was happy with the state of funds but was going to ask the members at the AGM to support a 5% increase in subscriptions. The kennels required repairs to the roof and some concreting needed renewing. Richard Randall, Mark Melvin and Richard Pain had made a handsome profit on the Hunt Ball, Christopher Latham again offered to run a mid-summer barbecue. Roy Lawrence had become the hunt BFSS representative and the Master now announced she had invited him to become joint master with her from the 1st April. Roy was the first joint master since Tony Hawkins had resigned in 1976.

The Devon & Somerset Staghounds were in the news having been served with a summons for trespass and the Mid Essex sent off a small donation to them which was gratefully accepted.

Phemie ,two whips and hounds (Clive Petchey Collection)

Michael Mason lost his joint meet secretary, Matthew Pain, who was away to London, and so Roy Lawrence offered to help with the meets. At the AGM Phemie stated in her usual staccato way the bad weather had cut hunting to 19 days with a tally of 19 brace. there had been gales and floods and she maintained the staying power of hounds was down to good breeding with all hounds being able to get out of the van at the end of all meets, though she doubted whether the same could be said for all the members or followers!

Carded meets for the 1986/7 season were in the ratio of 16 of the old country meets to 20 in the new extended country and beyond. For an opening meet the White Horse, Mundon had been chosen, but the Fox, Mashbury for the close.

In 1987 Barry Clark gave up as Chairman and Clive Petchey took over. Roy Lawrence, who had been made Joint Master by Phemie in the previous year, had retired and moved down to Somerset so he now felt he had to resign as it was unlikely he would be up in Essex very often. He still turns out occasionally with his local pack. Roy remembers when whipping in collecting hounds with Phemie at Spurriers only to find Tony Hawkins had taken the hound van to deliver some cases of wine. The meet was at Writtle. Phemie decided there was no alternative but to take hounds on foot. To Roy's horror Phemie jogged all the way to the meet and a very hot and perspiring Roy manfully trundled after her. On arrival Phemie called out her apologies for her lateness and, to Roy's despair, announced the hunt would move off immediately.

Phemie was alone once more as sole Master after Roy moved. At the AGM it was pointed out by the chairman she had contributed nearly a four figure sum towards kennel expenses during the previous 14 months, no mean contribution. A hunt supper at Sandon and the Hunt Ball were both successful, for in regard to the latter Matthew Pain and Mark Melvin had between them sold 150 tickets and it only needed another 50 to make a reasonable profit. There was no doubt the younger members were whole heartedly supporting the hunt and their contribution to the revenue of the hunt was pro rata spectacular. Richard Randall had organised a Christmas Supper which had been enthusiastically attended.

Each year there was an Inter Hunt Quiz held at a hall in Maldon and every year the Mid Essex fielded a team on the stage. Sometimes the questions were kind to them , occasionally they were diabolical – the award of the wooden spoon had been known, but with the help of a Whip designate, young Ken Bartlett, that season the team had cruised through to win the shield. He had a phenomenal knowledge of hunts and hunting in general which overpowered the opposition and raised broad grins on the Mid Essex faces in the audience. Ken finally became a Joint Master of the Trinity Foot Beagles.

The Master's report at the AGM was interesting. 24 days hunting and a few Wednesdays in addition had accounted for 9 brace; Michael Mason had taken over as joint Meet Secretary with Jim Hocking, and Phemie said Peter Spital was doing sterling remedial work at the kennels where she now had $17\frac{1}{2}$ couple (some new hounds having been drafted in), and 3 couple of pups. She also pointed out she was a 'working Master, not social'. She was rebuilding the pack.

The Hound List for 1987/8 actually read as follows:

Dogs		Bitches	
Briton	82 OBB	Gossip	87
Binder	86 ALD	Glamour	87
Gangster	87	Glitter	87
Gunner	87	Jasmine	80
General	87	Junket	80
Joker	80	Joyful	80
Jester	80	Susan	77
Justice	80	Saintly	77
Janitor	80	Spangle	79
Surgeon	77	Spitfire	79
Spartan	79	Friendly	81
Spokesman	79	Fathom	81
Sportsman	79	Fashion	82
Flagman	81	Warbler	77
Farmer	81		
Foreman	82		
Fencer	82		
Forester	86 ALD		
Woodman	86 ALD		
Waiter	86 ALD		
Wizard	86 ALD		

Doghounds 10¹/₂ couple   Bitches 7 couple

Puppies whelped Easter Day 1987

Jupiter   Judgement
Jackdaw   Juno
Jaunty   Jigsaw
Jewellery

Legend: OBB – Old Berkeley Beagles, ALD – Aldershot Beagles

Now came the crunch! The Treasurer's report in the AGM quoted a deficit of £1514 as against £340 in the previous year. Expenditure was up due to veterinary fees on the breeding programme, a not unusual phenomena where pups are concerned and often a matter of luck. He also made reference to the Master having an injury to her thumb, though the minutes make no further elaboration regrettably. It must have curtailed her activities for a period. The response was an increased subscription yet again to £120 a single, £150 a family, (less £20 and £15 respectively if paid up by the end of July 1987), OAPs and under 25s – £30, cards £10. Plus a 'Thumb Fund' surcharge of £25! Sonny Davey, ever a friend loyal to the hunt, produced an exceedingly handsome and much appreciated donation to funds, and from America there came $150 from an enthusiastic Anthony Garvin who had spent a day out with the pack the previous season, so there was some hints of light in the gloom of the storm clouds.

Under any other business it is noted that meet times had been altered to 1130 for 1200, and 1030 when hounds now met on alternate Wednesdays: an open afternoon at kennels was to be arranged, another hunt ball, barbecue, at last the Farmers' Supper to be resurrected, a hunt supper, a Clay Pigeon Shoot and a Fish and Chip Supper.

By November 1987 funds were once more critical and much depended upon the success of the hunt ball and other fund raising functions. Meets were arranged by Michael Mason without the help of Jim Hocking who had suffered an accident, so Michael was looking desperately for someone else to assist for the time being; however, by January 1988 Jim Hocking was back helping Michael to arrange meets.

Prior to the opening meet, which took place at Limbourne Park on the 7th November 1987,there were 6 or 7 early morning meets and thereafter meets on Saturdays were at 11.30 am and on Wednesdays at 10.30 am, but by January 1988 Saturday meets were altered to 12 noon. It is of interest to see that on the season's meet cards only five of the meets were south of the A414 from the M11 to Maldon: the retreat northwards had begun as the density of traffic and building had increased in the south of the county to unreasonable proportions increasing the danger to hounds and field alike.

At the April 1988 Committee Meeting the Treasurer was feeling much more hopeful announcing that the current year would show a better balance than the previous year, the hunt ball having made a very good profit, and there would be no need to change the subscription. Peter Spital had already repaired the kennel roof and now undertook to reorganise the kennel runs' concrete surfaces and build a van carport out of old materials.

Michael Mason had arranged a supper at Hawkenden which was a success, whilst the hunt ball venue was being reconsidered. Christopher Latham had offered to run another barbecue, and Richard Randall a hunt supper. The Hunt Quiz team had dropped to 6th place. Sonny Davey had not been too well. The opening meet for the next season 1988/9 was fixed for Limbourne Park and by popular request the New Year meet was to be at Mashbury. Generally the meets were now more settled than in previous years: the meets below the A414 had dropped to four of which two were at Limbourne Park, Mundon.

The June AGM was to be preceded by a supper at The Grange where the meeting would be held, Barry and Brenda Clark once more acting as hosts. At the AGM it was mentioned that the Farmers' Supper was to be arranged in a different form. It was pointed out by Clive Petchey, the Chairman, so that the members should be aware the Master was subsidising hounds herself to a certain degree by settling some of the feed bills and he also listed specific work done by members as follows:

Michael Mason and Jim Hocking	Meets
Christopher Latham	Money Matters
Richard Randall	Social
Roger Flint	Secretary
Peter Spital	Kennel Engineering
Ken Bartlett	General Kennel Duties
Paul Schneidau	Counting hares and mechanical work
Richard Pain	Wednesday Meet Co-ordinator
Brenda Clark	Puppy walker and occasionally Wednesday whip

A diverse division of labour, indeed. However, changes were in the offing for Roger Flint gave up as Secretary and Roy Rodwell was elected in his stead, with a promise of help from David and Barbara Goldsmith; Mark Melvin and Matthew Pain retired from the committee though they would still continue to give support for the hunt ball. (Roy had quite a singing voice and tongue in cheek Tony Kidd proposed the minutes of the AGM should be set to music and sung by Roy at the next Christmas Supper.)

The Master was worried about the deer problem and it had now become essential before each meet to clear deer if hunting was not to be disrupted. Nevertheless she had 30 days hunting and only 2 blank days. A tally of 14.5 brace resulted. She also stressed the need for continued support from farmers.

The hound van had been replaced with donations totalling almost the full cost of the replacement so that only a small balance came out of general funds.

In Mid Essex

by
Roy Rodwell

In mid Essex near a pub
A van arrives this chilly winter morning
Hounds all jump out from the van
The Master bids them 'stay'
Then beaglers come out from the pub
And walk the hounds away
Then they all go hunting
On this chilly winter day
In mid Essex on a farm

In mid Essex in a field
The hunt is on, the hare is moving quickly
She races for a field away
The beagles they have cast
The Master she is running now
She hopes her breath will last
While beagles hurry on behind
The hare keeps going fast
In mid Essex on a farm

In mid Essex on a farm
Three hours of running over plough and stubble
The hare has gone – she got away
It was her lucky day
The beagles they are not around
They are nowhere to be seen
They boxed up half an hour ago
And are off to Clavering Green
From mid Essex on a farm

In Mid Essex – a song by Roy Rodwell

Mid Essex Beagles
December Lament

by
Roy Rodwell

Fifteen beagles all looked out
On a frosty morning
'Will we hunt or will we not'
Now the day is dawning
Eagerly they wait a call
From their Lady Master
'Hunting on – we meet at ten
May the hounds run faster'

Have beaglers got it right
Somewhere west of Beeleigh?
Or perhaps they all should be
South of Chignall Smealey
Hounds and Master rode along
Travelling from the West
To a venue of their own
The Rose and Crown Hartest

The Moral of this story is
Know where you should be going
The hunting venue will not change –
As long as it's not snowing !

TUNE: Good King Wenceslas

December Lament by Roy Rodwell

Michael Mason, Ken Bartlett and Phemie with hounds casting at Beyton Hall, Suffolk. (Hester Davies Collection)

Limbourne Park, Mundon 19th November 1994. (Hester Davies Collection)

On the 7th June 1988 the hunt lost one of its keen supporters. Reg Pratt died. For 6 years he had followed hounds, right up until the previous December and everyone was sad to hear of his death, he was a very enthusiastic beagler and had a broad sense of humour. Another death reported in the year was that of Tony Dunford Hawkins, the original Joint Master of the pack with Bill Knight.

Over the next twelve months, prior to the 1989 AGM Ken Bartlett was sending in reports to Bailey's Hunting Directory and Hound Magazine. A Clay Pigeon shoot at Ingatestone was held with the assistance of the Puckeridge Foxhounds Supporters Club (for which reciprocal help was to be given later) and

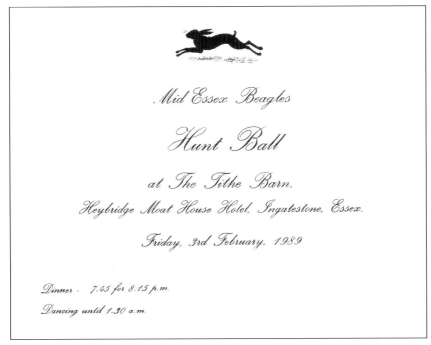

Mid Essex Beagles

Hunt Ball

at The Tithe Barn,
Heybridge Moat House Hotel, Ingatestone, Essex.

Friday, 3rd February, 1989

Dinner - 7.45 for 8.15 p.m.

Dancing until 1.30 a.m.

Hunt Ball Invitation

this turned out to be a very wet affair, not nearly as profitable as expected, making only £150 for the Mid Essex.

At the AGM it was announced that Christopher Latham wanted to move abroad, and was giving up the post of Treasurer: Richard Pain took over and Christopher was elected vice-chairman. The season had given the Master 39 days' hunting and 15 brace of hares were accounted for. Money, as usual, was a governing factor on the agenda and after much discussion a revolutionary idea was put forward and passed by a small majority, namely, that the annual subscription should be reduced to £100 and members should pay an additional cap of £5 per day.

Unfortunately, no committee minutes are available between the 1989 and 1990 AGMs. The Master reported at the 1990 AGM that she had 31 days hunting and a tally of 10½ brace were killed. Kennels held 19½ couple of hounds, one having been acquired from the Shropshire Beagles. All hounds were healthy and the situation on obtaining meat was good. She had invited John Bucknall to wear a green coat in view of his efforts in the field. The treasurer said the new subscription coupled with the £5 cap was working well but a good turnout for the hunt ball was essential to replenish funds.

An interesting problem arose for the Meet Secretaries. Apparently most farmers now wanted 2 to 3 months notice of hounds meeting on their land owing to previous misunderstandings. Michael Mason had to take this into consideration, no easy matter for a Meet Secretary trying desperately to organise a calendar of meets, with reminder cards going out 2 to 3 weeks before the actual

Fairstead 1992. L. to R. Barry Clark, Ruth Pain, Christopher Latham, Richard Randall, and David Goldsmith. (Hester Davies Collection)

meet. The meets carded for 1989/90 once again shewed 4 meets in the old original country and the rest further north.

During the 1990/1 season there were quite a few meets before the New Year that were changed after the meet card had been issued, though without spoiling it in any way despite two Suffolk meets being cancelled. In January there was a meet at the Red Rose, Lindsay Street , Monks Eleigh 'then onward to Boyton Hall for hunting … tea afterwards.' Thus the amended meets notice read. Again after the start of 1991 many of the meets had to be changed, but the substitutions were more than adequate.

When the next committee meeting was held on the 28th May 1991 it was seen that the Christmas supper was a success but by comparison the hunt ball, which was a joint effort with the Newmarket Beagles, was not. There had been insufficient support on ticket sales and there was doubt with respect to the choice of band. Both Christopher Latham and Jim Hocking resigned from the committee after a long period of service and their help and assistance was much missed. Funds as usual were once more the vexing question: Richard Pain needed more to pay the bills for the next season and the subscription was to be £120 and the £5 cap for each meet attended. It was decided not to have a hunt ball.

Jim Hocking died in January 1992, and at his funeral in Colchester a large number of beaglers gathered and a poignant 'Gone away' was blown on the horn. His long association with the pack right from the start as whip, secretary, meet secretary and general adviser , even once as huntsman, had been of great value to the hunt.

The hunt were still sending a team to the annual hunt quiz at Maldon and this time they came second.

That year the AGM (the 40th) was more of a financial exercise than ever for there was a deficit of £99. Problems were the decrease in membership, so increased subscriptions might be an answer or disbandment. No one wanted the latter and so the subscription once more was raised, this time to £150 minimum plus £5 cap. It was a chicken and egg situation. A new idea of charging newcomers a subscription of £50 for the first season plus £5 field cap as an incentive to join was agreed. Gloom was in the air: the meet secretary was having trouble in organising meets during the shooting season. Some syndicates did not

Willingale 1993 (Hester Davies Collection)

Almost one year later, same place the following season. (Hester Davies Collection)

fix their shooting dates until a week before causing the cancellation of beagle meets at short notice, a frustration the meet secretary could well do without. The time of meets were to be altered. For a trial period hounds would meet at a farm or other location (map reference to be given on the meet card) at 10 a.m. and hunting to finish at approximately 1.30 p.m. This was a remarkable innovation. In fact, at the September committee meeting this was to continue until the 28th November without benefit of ale! The Boxing Day meet was to be at 12 noon at The Star, Good Easter, lubrication once more the norm.

During the 1991/2 season hounds had killed 6 brace of hare in 32 days hunting, the tally being smaller due to bad scenting. The meets carded were

A beaglers' tea at the Carrs, Limbourne Park (Clive Petchey Collection)

noticeably in farmyards or similar venues until mid-November when the usual more public meets at pubs were listed. In December there was a joint meet with the Albany Basset Hounds. The Mid Essex cracked off first with a 9.30 am start at Scaldhurst Farm Camp, Canewdon and after 1,30 pm it was the Albany's turn starting from the Bell, Purleigh. For obvious reasons the two packs could not hunt together.

In the following season 5½ brace of hares were accounted for in the same number of days hunting. Some more pups had been bred in kennels and Phemie Angus was very pleased with them. There is no opening meet mentioned on the first meet card for the season covering the 17th October to the 26th December, but the first meet at 1130 am on a Saturday was at the Queens Head, Hawkedon, by invitation; the next non-early meet was at 12 noon on the 26th December at the Star, Good Easter. However, thereafter for 1993 meets were at 10 am whatever the day. On the 20th February the meet was at 1130 am as it was to be at Park Farm, Scarning, near East Dereham in Norfolk, the home of Charles Farnham by invitation as it was within the Norfolk Beagles' country.

The treasurer in the June 1993 AGM was able to show a profit as against the previous year's deficit. He reckoned the success of a Kennel Open Day, a new innovation, to be the main profit factor. Nevertheless, the cost of hunting now ran at about £5,600 a year. Later in the summer Roz Ackland had organised a very successful Dog and Hound Show. She had already done much for the hunt in reducing the feed bill during the year. Attendance at a Boot Fair had also produced a profit.

The end of the financial year shewed a deficit larger than the previous season's profit, so by the June AGM in 1994 the estimated cost of running the pack had risen to £6,000 a year. The 10 o'clock start for meets was to continue, the problem of having to change meets due to shoots on the same dates of which the meet secretary received short notice still caused concern, though on the credit side another enjoyable joint meet with the Albany Bassett Hounds had taken place. The Master had 33 hunting days, 8 being lost as a result of wet conditions, and 5½ brace of hares was the tally. Interestingly, the number of hares had increased in the Chignall Smealy area, whilst the number of areas in which the pack could hunt in Essex were decreasing. To everyone's delight one of Hester Davies's photos of Mid Essex hounds had made a place for itself in the 1995 Airdale Beagles Calendar; not quite as adventurous as the WI, but nevertheless subsequent sales of the calendar among friends and members helped to swell funds.

In September the Chairman sent out a letter to members and potential supporters with suggested reduced subscriptions for limited hunting during the season. (Membership stood at 17.) It was realised not everyone could get out all the time to utilise a full member's subscription. In effect it would be possible in the category of supporter to pay just £30 for 5 days hunting, or for 15 days £85 for an individual (£130, family). During the season the usual urge to raise funds was at its peak: it looked as if funds would be sufficient until March. The kennels required concreting, creosoting and window repairs, with a nasty bill for rates being queried. One of the matters to be ironed out was the too frequent use of certain meet venues and it became necessary to revive some old ones or seek new meets. In April 1995 it was clear there would be a deficit for the 1994/5 season of about £500: the annual cost had risen to about £7,000. On a more cheerful note Dan and Marion Squier had raised £400 at Doggetts hosting a lunch with a tour of the farm afterwards for those still able to move, and the Mid Essex team won the Hunt Quiz for the second time at Maldon under the captaincy of Ken Bartlett.

Hounds scenting a line at Mashbury 18th March 1995 (Hester Davies Collection)

Great Stambridge, Barton Mill Meet – Peter Spital, Phemie, Julia, Ian and Michael Mason running to catch up having brought on a stray hound. (Hester Davies Collection)

Sadly Frank (Sonny) Davey died in January 1995. He had been failing for some time and had been a great friend and generous benefactor to the hunt, his active hunting with the pack going right back to its beginning, whether wearing green coat and whip in hand or wearing tweeds and sporting a thumb stick as in later life, he would turn out whenever health and the opportunity worked hand in hand.

At the 1995 AGM Tony Kidd gave up acting as joint auditor of the accounts and A.Bailey took over. Tony had done this work for many years. As a result of the Chairman's letter in the previous September the number of subscribers had increased to 20 with 6 limited subscriptions. Ken Bartlett had been appointed Assistant Meet Secretary. 6 brace of hares was the total for the season during 34 days hunting. The hound van needed about £200 spent on it to pass the MOT and already there was a small deficit in funds at the end of the year of £68. but it was not thought necessary to increase the subscription, instead thoughts turned to advertising for new members, a suggestion that was turned down in later weeks when it was felt conditions were not at the time conducive to advertising. Again the thorny question of meets arose, for some were over used, others the Master did not wish to hunt, being areas where hounds had to be stopped time and time again, presumably because of road conditions, and new venues had yet to be found.

CHAPTER 7

Giving Puss Best – 2004, *The Final Year*

The 44th AGM was held on the 20th June 1996 when it was announced that Phemie Angus and Ken Bartlett had purchased a van jointly and it was on loan to the hunt. The weather during the season had been appalling with snow, frozen ground and fog resulting in hunting only 28 days and a tally of 8 brace resulting. The strawberry tea and a luncheon were cancelled, but for the second year running the Mid Essex team won the Hunt Quiz and the victorious team comprised the Master, Ken Bartlett, Clive Petchey, Brian Smith and Ian Beveridge. MEB walks were being held during the summer, a new inovation. Roz Ackland was still giving a lot of assistance in kennels by her weekly trip to the abattoir for the collection of tripes and refusing to claim expenses. Two foxhound packs, in whose country the Mid Essex hunted, received cheques towards the cost

Hunt's Farm, Shalford. Phemie with Roz Ackland. 28th February 1996 (Hester Davies Collection)

Chignall Smealy – Hounds on the scent.
(Hester Davies Collection)

Mashbury – Hounds at work.
(Hester Davies Collection)

of their point-to-point farmers' lunches as the hunt no longer held the traditional farmers' supper.

Finance was still a problem and for the third year there was a deficit, yet the subscription remained at £150, but this time there would be a £15 levy in an effort to offset the loss and a further £10 required towards the Campaign for Hunting. It was mooted that each member should bring a new potential member to a meet, that money could be raised by holding after hunt pub lunches, a car boot sale of unwanted items, and publicity among known pro-hunting people within the country.

Michael Mason, Joint Meet Secretary, had warned that there was a possibility of loosing three meets in Suffolk, and one in Essex was restricted, so that members would have to travel further, or else go back to some of the old Essex meets long since abandoned; and Wednesday meets might be restricted to one in four. By now, after 8 years as Secretary, Roy Rodwell had given up, a longish stint during which he had given his time generously and Geoff Dignum offered to take over. Geoff had been associated with the pack for many, many years so he knew for what he was letting himself in. Roy had made a name in the Mid Essex for the verse he compiled, often set to music, which he would sing to entertain the others at suppers held in aid of funds and much of which was a wry comment on beagling.

It was fairly obvious that a decline in full membership would dramatically reduce available funds for the year, and to cap it the hunt were expected to find £250 annually for the Campaign for Hunting, as well as the Association of Masters of Harriers and Beagles annual subscription of £65, and £25 a year for BFSS membership. The Association's subscription was understandable and at least one could see the benefits: though the other organisations were supposed to be of benefit, at best it was hard to see this at the time when funds were so difficult to acquire.

Worries about the rates to be paid on the kennels still persisted, for they were assessed for Unified Business Rates, and this seemed unfair, for in no way could the hunt be considered a business, let alone a venture with a view to profit. Unfortunately no evidence was forthcoming of other hunts being in a more favourable position so the assessment had to be accepted reluctantly. This was

19th December 1998 – Guy's Farm, Curling Tye.
(Hester Davies Collection)

Guy's Farm Curling Tye. (Hester Davies Collection)

typical governmental, bureaucratic stupidity, and not the only one hunting would suffer over the next eight years.

During March 1997 the Chairman sent out notice of a Special General Meeting to be held the following April, as the deficit was much larger and the hunt was in peril once more. At this meeting the Treasurer confirmed the cost of running the hunt was £6,000 per annum, which had been fairly constant for several years. The problem was lack of members for the numbers had dwindled; whilst it needed about 24 members paying out in subscriptions and daily caps about £250 a season, in actual fact the membership had fallen below 20. A £30 levy was immediately imposed on members. The Treasurer's view was that to make ends meet he needed 10 people to guarantee £400 each and suggested the way to do it would be to pay a subscription of £300 in two instalments plus the cap of £5 on at least 20 occasions, though this would still mean finding £2,000 from other sources. Richard Pain did receive 7 guarantees and another 12 members at the meeting offered £150 plus caps so he was almost home on his requirements for the next season and the meeting achieved its design. To implement the funds raffles, a sausage and cyder evening, and a cheese and wine evening were to be held, together with a visit to New Hall Vineyard: it was really a case of how long the members could hold out gastronomically.

When the AGM was held on the 1st July 1997 the Chairman announced Ken Bartlett had raised £400 with two Sunday luncheons, a creditable effort, and the levy was coming in. By then the Treasurer was feeling a lot happier; donations, and the Master not submitting a veterinary bill she had paid herself, considerably reduced the anticipated liabilities. Phemie was rather inclined to do this from time to time and members felt this was very generous of her, especially after all the work she put in looking after hounds in kennels as well as hunting the pack during the season. She also paid the levy demanded by the Association of Masters of Harriers and Beagles and contributions towards the cost of Farmers' Lunches held at the point-to-points by each of the foxhound packs over whose country the Mid Essex hunted. (It had been traditional for the Mid Essex to hold their own Farmers' Supper for many years right from the hunt's inception, but in recent years the committee in their wisdom decreed it an unaffordable non-event.)

For the 1996/7 season 42 meets were arranged by the joint meet secretaries, 14 of which were lost due to weather, but the remaining 28 provided a tally of 6$\frac{1}{2}$ brace of hares. There was still a difficulty with shooting dates though the meets were arranged in spite of this. More country had been opened up in the Dengie Hundred around Bradwell, home of St. Peter's Chapel built by St. Cedd, the Roman fort nearby that modern edifice the atomic power station, and the war-

Fairstead, Terling 1999. (Hester Davies Collection)

'Warbler with pups – 18th August 1999 – 'Gossamer', 'Ghostly', 'Golden' and 'Garland'. (Hester Davies Collection)

'Brewer' (Hester Davies Collection)

time RAF Coastal Command airfield. Scaldhurst Camp, between Ashendon and Canewdon was another newish venue.The Quiz team came 4th! Richard Randall had to give up as Social Secretary, a post to which he had given much and for some years the hunt had benefitted greatly from his ability to run various money making ventures. A new Social Secretary would have to be found, and soon.

On the 30th June 1998 the 46th AGM was held. The car boot sale for which the Clarks had long stored the offerings from members was at last held and raised £30. Christopher and Jacqueline Latham had moved out of Essex to Buckinghamshire and unfortunately they would not be able to attend meets so often. For many years they had hosted social events or meetings in their home, before and after the tragic fire which burned Place Farm, Doddinghurst to the ground, they had organised hunt balls and Christopher had been treasurer for some years. Now the Mid Essex would have to cope without them.

Peter Spital became Vice-Chairman and Suzanne Brooking became the new Social Secretary. Early in 1999 Charles Farnham died. He had supported the Mid Essex from its early days arranging farmers' Suppers at the Half Way House on the Southend Arterial Road and often hunting twice a week until he sold his farm and bought another at Scarning in Norfolk when his visits were curtailed somewhat, though he managed a considerable number of meets each season despite the distance, and arranged the only visit to Norfolk. Yet another even more 'ancient' of the hunt died that year, Bill Knight, founder of the Hornchurch Beagles and first joint master with Tony Hawkins of the Mid Essex, well into his nineties; also, regrettably, Mrs. K. Rodwell, wife of Roy Rodwell (a former Secretary), who had loyally supported the pack ever since her husband became a member.

Richard Pain still had the unenviable task of struggling to keep the hunt viable for the 1999-2000 season. The Campaign for Hunting levy was biting into funds really needed to support hounds, and had it not been for solid work on the part of Julia Porter in assiduously collecting caps at meets funds would have been non-existent by the end of the financial year in 1999. Arising from the ashes, the Eastern Counties Otterhounds had re-appeared as mink hounds and it was intended to continue a good relationship with them in the future. After all, their history had been bound up with that of the Mid Essex in the past, not just by sharing kennels alone.

The 47th AGM held on the 15th June 1999 was significant. Clive Petchey, due to illness, had resigned as Chairman and his place was taken by Peter Spital. Clive had been Chairman for 12 years during a period of financial crises following one upon the other, in themselves guaranteed to make a chairman's life hard. He still remained a staunch member despite his physical problems and accepted the post of Vice-Chairman. Phemie announced she had invited Ian and Julia Porter to be Joint Masters with her: this was enthusiastically received by the members at the meeting. From Phemie's point of view, Julia had whipped in almost continuously since her younger days before she married Ian, and knew hounds well and Phemie's method of hunting, and helped in fund raising and committee work in addition, whilst Ian had cast his lot in with the beagles both before and after the marriage, so together they had a distinguished record with the hunt. They were a popular choice and could give solid backing to Phemie when she most needed it; now was a particularly difficult period as Phemie gave provisional notice of her intention to give up her mastership in two years time. It had long been her promise to the Committee that in the event of her wishing to cease hunting she would give them sufficient notice in advance, and this she

Retirement presentation to Clive Petchey – L. to R, Ruth Pain, ?, Liz Porter, Hester Davies, ?, Julia Porter, Clive holding the portrait of a Hare, Brenda Clark, Barry Clark, Roy Rodwell, Ian Porter, and Richard Pain, also two four legged followers, parentage unknown. (Clive Petchey Collection)

did. Everyone realised this was provisional and secretly hoped there would be a possibility that this might not be the end.

The tally at the end of the 1998/9 season was 5½ brace. The joint Meet Secretaries were hopeful that there might be 'double days', presumably as distinct from true joint meets, where one pack would hunt in the morning and another in the afternoon: it was hoped these could be arranged with the Stour Valley Beagles, the Albany Basset Hounds and the Eastern Counties Mink Hounds. There was also a chance of opening up that part of the Essex Farmers and Union country north of the River Crouch and its estuary (east of Woodham Ferrers and west of Bradwell), and holding more meets in the East Essex Foxhounds country already registered with the Mid Essex. There were good possibilities for the next season.

Suzanne Brooking as Social Secretary confirmed £313.34 had been raised by various events, and Hester Davies had raised £64 by the production and sale of Christmas cards. Nevertheless, funds were down once more and a deficit of £944 had to be overcome. The Campaign for Hunting levy was still crippling the pack, and so, too, the loss of some members, a hazard ever present due to people moving out of the country, or dying. To counteract the situation the Members agreed to the subscription being raised to £175 plus a daily cap of £7.

For some time the Association had been recommending that hunts should have a written constitution in accordance with new rules, so a draft was prepared by the Chairman after Richard Randall had perused the model supplied by the Association, and this was to be supplied to the members and then discussed at the next AGM in the year 2000.

Someone at the meeting raised the point that the Treasurer should be correctly described as Book Keeper, as his function did not include fund raising. Could this be the ugly head of political correctness insinuating itself into the Beagles? A more fatuous choice, a more denigrating description of the Treasurer's efforts could not be contemplated. It is quite clear that a Treasurer's job is to collect moneys to keep the pack solvent, to warn if funds are short and to advise methods of raising further moneys, to forward budget for the following season, but in no way could he be described as a mere book keeper. It always has been for others to raise funds at the recommendation of the Treasurer. Richard Pain and all his predecessors had used their best endeavours during the whole time that the pack was in existence to carry out their duties as Honourary Treasurers to the full.

Phemie with her sister Wendy, 'Muffin' and 'the Shropshire Lads' (Clive Petchey Collection)

By March 2000 the Treasurer was feeling more optimistic and forecasting a surplus by the end of the season; the membership had risen to 20 and the Hunting Levy for the year was being paid. When the AGM came round in June the Treasurer, still the optimist, kept the subscription at £175 but agreed that subscribers would pay only a £5 cap whilst non-members were expected to pay £7. One factor which contributed towards the easing of the funds was the payment of vetinary bills by the joint masters. Clive Petchey now decided to relinquish his vice-chairmanship. Meet cards would announce that followers should meet at 10.15 am to move off at 10.30 am in the future, though for distant meets this might be amended to allow hunting to commence at 11 am. By now the followers enjoyed a few hours hunting and then relaxed in a pub over lunch; quite different from the earlier days when hounds met at 11.30 am and tea at a pub followed about 3 pm or later, dependant upon whether all hounds were in the van, so it was not unusual for someone to make up plates of sandwiches and cakes to ensure the Master and whips, who might be out until dark collecting the odd straggler, had something.

Again the matter of a constitution was raised but held over for the next committee meeting. The pack hunted for 31 days, loosing 4 to frost and one to fog. The tally was 8 brace. It had been a better season than had been seen for some years. The Joint Meet secretaries were much involved with farmers, foxhound packs, shoot managers, gamekeepers and wildfowlers in order to

Pups. (Phemie Angus Collection)

More Pups. (Phemie Angus Collection)

Phemie coupling hounds preparatory to morning
exercise (Colin Miller Collection)

Off to exercise. (Colin Miller Collection)

Hampton Barns, Great Stambridge – 22nd January 2000, still 6 couple preparing to move off (Hester Davies Collection)

Shellow Cross, near Roxwell – 29th January 2000, Barry and Brenda Clark with Phillip Schneidau and Roy Rodwell during a short break. (Hester Davies Collection)

The upwardly mobile beagler – Ken Bartlett, 2000, slightly feeling his age! (Hester Davies Collection)

produce decent meet cards for the season; no easy matter, and Michael Mason and Ken Bartlett had done well for the hunt.

Later in the year a swine fever outbreak was notified. Geoff Dignum gave up as Secretary and Mr and Mrs Brooking were moving from the area and gave their resignations. Suzanne Brooking and her husband had done much for the beagles, she as Social Secretary, he as Auditor, and together they had organised a successful buffet lunch at the Green Man, Little Waltham and offered their house for the AGM to be held in September, later than usual because of the outbreak which could put the opening of the hunting season back until late November. The Treasurer was facing a deficit mainly due to a reduction in members to 17 with a loss in cap money from meets not held due to foot and mouth restrictions, 6 or 7 had been lost, and it looked as if the position would be grave as to the future. It was felt that the committee would no longer be able to raise sufficient funds for the everyday running of the pack. The Chairman wrote to the members informing them of the position in August prior to the 49th AGM on the 18th September 2001.

Apparently hunting had taken place in the 2000/1 season on 20 days during which 4½ brace had been caught, the pack then consisting of 6 couple of doghounds and 4½ couple of bitches. During the season Suzanne Brooking had whipped in and also Noel and Rosemary Watson. The potential in Dengie Hundred was quite good for there were new tenants of the land but hunting was suspended by the Government as from the 22nd February due to Foot and Mouth which stopped hunting for the rest of the season. In fact, all point-to-points, shooting and coursing were suspended as well, and the joint Meet Secretaries forecast no hunting before Christmas which would hit the 2001/2 season. It was anticipated that moneys would run out by February 2002 by the latest, after which the pack could no longer be supported. Despite the facts as put forward it was decided to carry on and Hester Davies was appointed Secretary with Noel and Rosemary Watson as Social Secretaries and Barry Clark was now to be the sole auditor.

By November 2001 there was hopes of hunting resuming in January 2002. However, DEFRA had produced rules and regulations based on the Animal Health Act 1981 requiring hunting permits to be obtained by hunts which included approval of meet venues and each participant was expected to sign a certificate of compliance giving the vehicle registration number of any vehicle to be brought to the meets and it was necessary to disinfect wheels, wheel arches and other parts of the vehicle likely to come into contact with the disease. The Government had reacted slowly, but the draconian, ruthless erradication had started. This put a difficult task before hunt secretaries in general and made the 2001/2 season a nightmare for them. The whole cumbersome system evolved by

Guests at the party – Brenda Clerk, Richard Pain, Barbara Goldsmith, Jim Hocking, Ruth Pain, Peter Blacklock, standing at back Philip Schneidau, Barry Clark and Suzanne Brooking (Phemie Angus Collection)

Phemie's Birthday Party. Unwrapping a present (Hester Davis Collection)

a government department with its back to the wall was irrational, unnecessary and merely an excuse for attempting to place controls on hunting. Nothing like this had ever been used as a curb before, and in all the history of animal disease outbreaks previously in living memory there had been no need for such regulatory practice: common sense had always prevailed in the past.

There was some hunting in 2002 to complete the season under these stringent requirements but subsequently hounds were hunted by the Joint Masters as a private pack without the aid of a committee and Arthur Ringe hunted hounds occasionally. There was no hunting for the Mid Essex during the 2003/4 season, and in March 2004 Phemie reluctantly informed the Director of the Association of Masters of Harriers and Beagles, the relevant governing body, that the Mid Essex Beagles would be disbanding forthwith, and wrote the following letter to the members and friends of the hunt:

Dear

I have been with the Mid Essex Beagles for 53 seasons and since 1955 I have had the honour of carrying the horn. I have always been most splendidly supported by our whippers-in – whatever the weather!

Captain & Mrs Hawkins retired to Wales in 1967 when the breeding and maintenance of the hounds became my responsibility. After temporary accommodation with the Eastern Counties Otterhounds and later the Trinity Foot Beagles the hounds were moved to Black Lodge in 1979 where they remain. Our local friends and farmers took the beagles to their hearts and are always ready to assist in any difficulties. The local children particularly loved to help with the puppies (the children are now married and some with their own little ones!)

We have now decided to close the M.E.B. at the end of this season. This has been a very difficult decision to reach and has involved much careful consideration and even sadness.

The main problem has been finding meets that are safe to hunt. Fast traffic, new roads and increased urbanisation are not a recipe for safe hunting. In 1952 we had 68 different meets but we now have only 7 or 8 which are still safe. We have only been able to keep these going due to the support of the Farmers, Landowners, Shoot Owners and their ever helpful Keepers. We are also very indebted to the three Packs of Foxhounds and the Blackwater Wild Fowlers Association. It has only been through the help and support of all these friends that our two meet secretaries have been able to keep us hunting. None of this has been helped by the mismanagement over foot & mouth and all the other problems facing Farming.

The hounds are being kept on at Black Lodge and are looking fit and well and it is hoped that they will remain here for the rest of their lives.

According to the rules of the Association of Masters of Harriers and Beagles which the M.E.B., like all other beagle packs, belong, we will have to formally relinquish our country at the end of the season. This means that another pack may decide to register the country, in which case, they will have to approach everyone concerned as the M.E.B. will no longer be involved.

At this very sad time, my two joint masters and I would very much like to take this opportunity of thanking all those who have made the existence of the M.E.B. possible. Many people have contributed in many ways over the years, far too numerous to mention, but we hope you are all left with happy memories; as we shall be.

Yours sincerely

Phemie Angus

Miss J.E.H.Angus

The luncheon after disbandment. Phemie cuts the cake. (Clive Petchey Collection)

Henry & Janet Marriage at the luncheon.
(Author's Collection)

Dan & Marion Squier at the luncheon.
(Author's Collection)

Going Home (Clive Petchey Collection)

*Julia presents the MEB silver salver to C. Proctor MH Claro Beagles 22 July 04 at the Peterborough
Hound Show (Hester Davies Collection)*

EPILOGUE

The Association decided that it would purchase a silver salver, to be called the Mid Essex Silver Salver, for presentation each year at the Peterborough Hound Show to the beagle pack that had done most for the promotion of beagling during the year. Julia Porter presented it for the first time on the 22nd July 2004 to Mr. C. Proctor MH of the Claro Beagles.

Thus the Mid Essex Beagles ended. It was before the ban in February 2005. Some may think it would have been better to wait for the ban to take effect: others may think it right that, having come to the end of good country, so necessary for beagling , it was the proper thing to do. Perhaps one day someone will apply to the Masters of Harriers and Beagles Association to re-open the country, or at least part of it, in whatever form permitted by law, and one hopes it will be during the lifetime of some of the old followers of the Mid Essex Beagles who may be persuaded to give of their knowledge and experience to help the new beaglers enjoy a little of what, for many, has been a way of life and a fuller understanding of nature.

The hare will still remain a mysterious creature, independant and at times appearing feckless but full of courage. *Floreat lepus.*

ACKNOWLEDGMENTS

I would like to thank the following for allowing me to select photographs from their collections:

Phemie Angus
Hester Davies
Brenda Clark
Jim Meads, for very kindly allowing me to use some photographs taken by his late father
Colin Miller
Clive Petchey

I would also like to thank the following:

Phemie Angus, for encouragement throughout and her witty anecdotes.
Julia Porter, without whom the book might never have appeared in print.
Liz Porter, for a host of reminiscences.
My wife Barbara, for encouragement and patience.
Clive and Pam Petchey, for their anecdotes and general assistance.
Tony Kidd, for producing documents and old papers relating to the hunt.
Colin Miller, for his recollections, especially of hunting in Wales.
Roy Lawrence, his recollections were of great help.
John Baddeley, with respect to his late father.
Geoff Dignum, for his stories, including the Welsh trips.
Roy Rodwell, for allowing me to reproduce two of his songs.
Peter Spital, for access to old minutes of meetings held by him.
Mrs. E.A. Salmon, Director of the Association of Masters of Harriers and Beagles for permission to reproduce part of the Association's Map of Countries.

APPENDICES

Appendix A

Office Holders Mid Essex Beagles

MASTERS:

William Knight	1947–1958
Capt. Anthony C.C. Dunford Hawkins	1952–1976
Mrs. Esther Dunford Hawkins	1958–1967
Miss P. Angus	1967–2004
Roy Lawrence	1986–1987
Mrs Julia Porter	1999–2004
Dr. Ian Porter	1999 –2004

CHAIRMEN:

David Baddeley	1953–1971
Frank Fitzwilliam	1971–1976
Peter Hopton	1976–1979
Barry Clark	1979–1987
Clive Petchey	1987–1999
Peter Spital	1999–2002

SECRETARIES:

Simon Casey	1953–1955
Jim Hocking	1955–1965, 1987–1988 (JT)
Eric Dix	1958 –1959 (JT)
Colin Miller	1958–1977
Mrs. Terry Miller	1965–1967 (JT)
Derick Carlisle	1969–1977 (Meets)
Peter Bostridge	1977–1983
Roger Flint	1980–1988 (JT)
Mark Melvin	1983–(Meets)
Matthew Pain	–1986 (Meets)
Roy Rodwell	1988–
Roy Lawrence	1986–1987 (Meets)
Michael Mason	1990 –2002 (Meets)
Geoff Dignum	–2000
Ken Bartlett	1994–2002 (Meets)
Miss Hester Davies	2000–2002

KENNEL HUNTSMEN:

Arthur Whittaker	1953–1953
Bill Kat	1953–1965
Clive Knott	1965–1967
Vic Ramsay	1967–1967
Bob Street (ECOH)	1967–1967
Derek Gardner (ECOH)	1967–1974
Jack Poyle (TFB)	1974–1976
John Calder (TFB)	1976–1979

WHIPS:

Miss Phemie Angus	1953–1956
Jim Hocking	1947–1970
John Pertwee	1947–
Simon V.N.Casey	1947–
Frank (Sonny) Davey	1947–1985
F/Lt. P.Hart RAF	
Roy Lawrence	1959 –
Peter Hopton	1960 –
Julia Porter (Aspinall)	1968 – , and 1994–1999
Derek Carlisle	1976 (Weds)
Roderick Edwards	
Prof. F.W.Leaky	
Mark Melvin	
Michael Mason	1975–
Roderick Duncan	
Ken Bartlett	1987–2002
Peter Spital	1990–
J. Buckwell	1990–
Brenda Clark	(Weds)
Ian Porter	–1999
Mrs. Suzanne Brooking	2000–
Mr and Mrs R. Watson	2000–

TREASURERS:

Dick Richards	1953–1971
Miss Lovell	1960–1962 (JT)
Peter Bostridge	1971–1977
Christopher Latham	1977–1989
Richard Pain	1989–2002

Author's Note
Some dates could not be verified and blanks
have been left.

Appendix B

Hounds

Pedigree: Sex: Dog   Name: Mid Essex Goblin   Bred by: Mid Essex Beagles   Whelped: 10th June 1999

Parents	Grandparents	Great Grandparents	Gt. Gt. Grandparents	Gt. Gt. Gt. G'parents
				CHRISTCH. Logman
			ALD. Warner'66	ALD. Pilot'60
		ALD. Packer'71		
			DUMMER Plover	DUMMER Baggage'59
	ME Joker'80			PARK Keswick'66
			ME Kernel'72	ME Gaylass'67
		ME Jaunty'75		RADLEY Loader'64
			ME Joyful'71	ME Jasmine'64
ME Gameboy'90				PARK Keswick'66
			TFB Sampson'72	CHRISTCH. Speedy'67
		ME Guardsman'78		ME Galloper'64
	ME Gossip'87		ME Glory'71	ME Jaunty'67
				ALD. Finder'77
		ME Friendly'81	ALD. Falstaff '79	ALD. Favourite'76
				ME Jester'67
ME Goblin'99			ME Stylish'73	TFB Stella'70
		ALD. Forager'82		
	ALD. Wizard'86			
		ALD. Woodbine'82		
ME Warbler				ALD. Warner'66
			ALD. Packer'71	DUMMER Plover
		ME Joker'80		ME Kernel'72
		ME Jaunty'75		ME Joyful'71
	ME Juno'88		ALD. Falstaff'79	ALD. Finder'77
				ALD. Favourite'76
		ME Friendly'81		ME Jester'67
			ME Stylish'73	TFB Stella'70

Legend: ALD: Aldershot CHRISTCH: Christchurch ME: Mid Essex TFB: Trinity Foot

Showing Hounds

Hounds were shown at Peterborough, Aldershot, Harrogate and Honiton, the shows to which Masters of Packs recognised by the Association could take hounds and compete. The Mid Essex obtained at least 55 placings (17 1st. prizes), including 2 doghound championships, one bitch hound championship and 4 reserve championships. The last hound shewn at Peterborough was MEB 'Gangway' in 1969, walked by the Fitzwilliams family. 'Gangway' was a descendant of MEB 'Gossip' '49 (see chart). He was placed first in the Unentered Doghound Class and judged by Philip Burrows MH and Maj. George Leake MH.

Breeding of Hounds

Phemie Angus has always attributed the origins of the pack she hunted and bred to three hounds: Christchurch 'Wishful' 1953, New College & Magdalen 'Gossip' 1949, and Newcastle 'Juno' 1955. As may be seen from the chart of MEB 'Goblin' above close line breeding was followed to produce a pack of distinction. The resultant placings at the hound shows mentioned above are indicative of the hard work put into breeding during the early years. Originally a tri-colour pack the light lemon and white gradually took its place and remained so at Capt. Hawkins's request when handing over hounds to Phemie Angus.

Appendix C

Mid Essex Beagles Meet Venues

Meet:	Pub:	Other venue:
Abbess Roding		Rookwood Hall
Abridge		
Bannister Green	The Three Horseshoes	Leighs Lodge
Barling Marsh		Mucking Hall
Battlesbridge	The Barge	Hayes Farm
Beauchamps		(Brown) East of Southend Airport, also Shopland Hall adjacent
Beazley End	The Cock	By invitation
Bicknacre	The Two Brewers	
Blackmore	The Bull	
Blackmore End	The Red Cow	Bakers Farm
Boreham	The Queen's Head	New Hall by invitation, Phillows Farm and Culvert's Farm Yard
Boreham Hall		By Invitation of Ford Motors
Bradwell		Eastlands Farm
Brent Pelham	Black Horse	By invitation
Bulphan Fen	The Harrow	
Burnham on Crouch	The White Hart	
Canewden	The Chequers	Also Scaldhurst Farm
Chignall Smealy	Pig & Whistle	Additional meet at Woodhall Farm
Chigwell Row		Thrift House, David Baddeley
Church End	Punch Bowl, Paglesham	
Clavering		By invitation
Cock Clark	The Plough	
Cranham	The Thatched House	The Jobbers Rest
Curling Tye Green		Guys Farm
Danbury Common	The Cricketers	Or at Sir Carne Rasch's house
Dengie Marshes		Turncole Farm
East End	The Plough & Sail, Paglesham	
East Hanningfield	The Windmill	East Hanningfield Hall
East Horndon		
Fairstead		Fairstead Hall Beet pad
Feering		
Fristling Hall		
Fuller Street		Met at beet pad at Fairstead Nr Terling
Galleywood		Parklands Farm
Good Easter	The Star	Black Barns when pub closed
Guestingthorpe		By invitation Delvyns
Gosfield		
Great Burstead		
Great Leighs	St. Anne's Castle	
Great Stambridge		Hampton Barns, Barton Hall
Hartest	The Crown	By invitation
Hawkendon	The Queens Head	By invitation
Herongate	Blue Boar	For Heron Hall
High Easter	The Fox? or Cock & Bell	
Hornchurch Aerodrome	Officers' Mess	
Horndon on the Hill	The Bell	Also Great Mulgraves (Jack Buckenham's)
Hutton Church		For Creasy's Farm
Ingatestone	The Bell	
Kelvedon		Felix Hall Leaping Wells
Lambourne End	The Beehive	
Latchingdon	The Lion	
Lindsey Tye		By invitation Boyton Hall
Little Baddow	The Rodney	

Meet:	Pub:	Other venue:
Little Burstead		Sudburys Farm
Little Leighs		Leez Priory
Little Waltham	One Bell	The White Hart
Littley Green	The Compasses	
Margaretting Tye	The White Hart	
Mashbury	The Fox	Bailey's Farm and Bards Hall
Mayland		Lawling Hall
Moreton	The Nag's Head or White Hart	Nether Hall
Mundon		Limbourne Park, Iltney Farm
Navestock Heath	The Green Man	
Nine Ashes	The Wheatsheaf	Also The Black horse
North Fambridge	The Ferry Boat	
Norton Heath		Spurriers
Nounsley	The Sportsman's Arms	
Ockenden, N	The Old White Horse	
Orsett	The Dog & Partridge	
Panfield	The Bell	
Paglesham	The Punchbowl	Church Hall
Paslow Common	The Black Horse	
Pleshey	The White Horse	
Purleigh	The Queen's Head	
Radley Green	The Cuckoo (previously The Thatchers)	
Radwinter	The Plough	By invitation
Rettendon	The Bell	
Rochford		Doggetts (Squiers'), Scaldhurst Farm and Temple Farm
Roxwell	The Cross Keys, The Chequers	Butthatch Farm, Hill Farm
Runsell Green	The Anchor, Danbury	
Sandon	The Crown	
Scarning, Norfolk		By invitation Park Farm, Charles Farnham
Shalford		Hunts Farm
Shalford Green	The Fox	
Shellow Bowells		Shellow Cross Farm
South Fambridge	The Anchor	
Southminster	The Queens Head	Upper Wycke and New Moor Farm
South Ockendon	(pub on the green)	Hunted towards Bulphan Fen
Stagdon Cross		Met on grass verge
Stambourne	The Red Lion	By invitation
Stanford Rivers	White Hart	
Stansfield	The Compasses	By invitation (near Hartest)
Stapleford Abbots	The Rabbits	Also Passingford bridge
Stebbing		By invitation White House Farm
Steeple		Batts Farm and Steeple Hall
Sutton Hall		East of Southend Airport (Steel)
Stock	The Compasses	
Stow Maries		Flanbirds Farm
Tanfield Tye		
Terling	Rayleigh Arms	Joint Meet with Newmarket Beagles and Fairstead Hall
Thistley Green		Leigh's Lodge
Tillingham		East Hyde Hall
Toot Hill	No meet	Tea at Green Man
Toppesfield		By invitation Berwick Hall Farm
Warley	The Headley Arms	
West Hanningfield	The Three Compasses	
West Horndon Station		

Meet:	Pub:	Other venue:
Weston Longville		By invitation Morton Hall
White Notley	The Plough	
Willingale	The Bell, Maltsters Arms	Spains Hall
Woodham Ferrers	The Bell	
Woodham Mortimer		Lodge Farm
Woodham Walter	The Cats	Guys Farm
Writtle		Writtle College

Appendix D

Biblography:

THE MID ESSEX BEAGLES
by B.G.E.Webster published by The Hunts Association (G.W. May, Ltd.)

BAILEY'S HUNTING DIRECTORY Publishers various

ASSOCIATION OF MASTERS OF HARRIERS AND BEAGLES Year Book

INDEX